Chrysanthemums

CHRYSANTHEMUMS
THE COMPLETE GUIDE

BADEN LOCKE

The Crowood Press

First published in 1990 by
The Crowood Press Ltd
Ramsbury, Marlborough
Wiltshire SN8 2HR

Paperback edition 1995

British Library Cataloguing in Publication Data

A catalogue record for this book is available from the British Library.

ISBN 1 85223 890 9

Acknowledgements

I wish to acknowledge the valuable assistance and information
given to me by the following: the National Chrysanthemum
Society; Mr George Freestone; Mr Richard Harris; Mr C. Riley;
Mr J. Woolman. Thanks especially to all my family, who have
encouraged me and given their time assisting in correcting and
editing. Most of all I would like to thank Margaret, my wife, who
has spent many hours reading and correcting the draft copy, and
who gave me the inspiration to take on and complete this book.

Picture Credits

Line artwork by Sophie Allington
Colour photographs by the author

Typeset by Footnote Graphics, Warminster, Wiltshire
Printed in Great Britain by Redwood Books, Trowbridge, Wiltshire

Contents

Foreword

With the possible exception of the rose, the chrysanthemum must be the most widely-grown flower throughout the world. With its many forms and colours and its long flowering period – outdoors from August until the first frosts, and under glass from November until January – the chrysanthemum really does merit the title bestowed on it by its devotees: 'Queen of the Autumn'! And professional chrysanthemum breeders can now, of course, produce chrysanthemums to flower all the year round.

I can think of no one better qualified to write for the amateur on the cultivation and exhibition of chrysanthemums than Baden Locke, the General Secretary of the National Chrysanthemum Society. He has been growing chrysanthemums since the mid-1950s, although pressures of work delayed the start of his exhibiting career until the early 1970s. Since then he has exhibited widely and has won major prizes at local, national and international shows. He has also been deeply involved in an administrative capacity with Rugby Chrysanthemum Society and the Midland Group of the National Chrysanthemum Society, and is now a Vice-President of both.

Baden's spare time has been dedicated to the chrysanthemum for over thirty years and his enthusiasm remains as keen now as when he started. This is quite evident from this book, and I am pleased to commend it wholeheartedly to all growers and exhibitors alike, whether expert or novice, as well as to those who have not yet experienced the pleasures of our rewarding hobby.

Larry Barlow
Chairman, National Chrysanthemum
Society Floral Committee

Introduction

The chrysanthemum, one of the most popular, intriguing and adaptable of plants, was first introduced into Britain in 1790, and since that date the hybridisers have gradually increased the size, shape and colour range to what we see today. The earliest chrysanthemums were late-flowering cultivars from which our modern-day early, mid-season and late cultivars have been bred. Within each category there are a number of sub-sections providing an abundance of colours and varying types of blooms that flower from early August through to October in the open ground, and throughout the year in the modern greenhouse. Ranging from the magnificent Japanese blooms measuring up to 12in (30cm) in diameter to the daisy-like charm pot plants capable of bearing several hundred small flowers, there is a chrysanthemum for all gardens.

The name chrysanthemum is derived from the Greek words *chrysos* (gold) and *anthos* (flower). The chrysanthemum family is represented in many plants throughout Europe, and is found in the British Isles in the common Ox-eye Daisy and Corn Marigold, but it is the species from China and Japan that is associated with Britain's cultivated chrysanthemums. Early travellers reported the cultivation of this flower by Chinese gardeners, and marvelled at the way it was trained into shapes depicting well-known figures. This art is still practised in Japan today.

The first recorded reference to the chrysanthemum was found in the writings of the Chinese philosopher Confucius about 500 BC, and for centuries this flower was cultivated for both medicinal purposes and decorative beauty.

In 1789 a French merchant, M. Blanchard, imported three plants from China, white, purple and violet; unfortunately only the purple plant reached France alive. In the following year plants of this cultivar arrived in England, the first large flower of this species to be known in Europe and often referred to as 'Old Purple' or 'Old Red'. Between 1798 and 1808 eight new cultivars were imported, and in 1802 'Old Purple' sported white, giving ten cultivars with a colour range of golden yellow, pale yellow, rose, buff, white and lilac, many with quilled petals. In 1823 another seventeen new cultivars were brought into Britain, bringing the number of cultivars to around thirty. The first flowers bore very little resemblance to present-day cultivars, being mostly the single quill petal type, with some semi-doubles and anemone centred, but gradually throughout the nineteenth century the hybridisers cross-bred and developed cultivars with characteristics similar to those of today.

The first recorded British seedling to be exhibited was in December 1832. It soon captured the hearts of thousands of amateur gardeners – from this period chrysanthemum societies were formed in most British cities and towns. The first incurving blooms appeared towards the middle of the nineteenth century, followed by the reflexing type, and then the large, long-petalled varieties from Japan. During this period gardeners began to exhibit their new varieties, and the popularity of the chrysanthemum caught the imagination of the general public, with the demand for plants growing rapidly.

The exciting changes that are taking place in the chrysanthemum world mean that the amateur raiser is now gradually taking on the breeding of new cultivars for exhibition from the professional nurseryman.

Chrysanthemums will flourish in practically any soil providing it is well drained, has sufficient nutrients to produce a steady growth and is kept free from the usual pests. Every garden has adequate sunlight for chrysanthemums, so it is fair to say that the chrysanthemum is not a fussy plant; in order to grow a first-rate bloom, however, attention must be paid to every little detail.

1

Beginning

WHICH TYPE OF CULTIVAR?

Having made the decision to grow chrysanthemums, you must consider where they are to be grown (in the open ground or in a greenhouse), as this decision determines the cultivar and type of cultivation necessary.

If you intend to grow early-flowering cultivars in beds in the open ground for purely decorative purposes or cutting, you should be looking for cultivars that will flower from early August through to the frosts in October, that are weather resistant and not too tall.

If the position chosen is in a border, then the ideal type is the new early-flowering charm ('cushion chrysanthemum') that grows from 10 to 15in (25 to 38cm) high and comes in various colours. On the other hand, if only a few plants are to be grown to provide blooms for cutting, then the ideal selection would be spray cultivars, which could be planted at the back of the border with taller plants and would give an abundance of cut blooms from August to mid-October. If, when selecting the cultivars to be grown, you remember that the height of the mature plants will vary from anything between 36 to 48in (90 to 120cm) tall, this will prevent disappointment later.

If the plants are for providing cut flowers in the latter part of the year and you have greenhouse facilities, you will require late-flowering cultivars, commonly known as greenhouse cultivars. These also come in a wide range of types, colours and heights, and like the early-flowering cultivars can be flowered over a long period from early October to late January. Those flowering in early October to early November usually require very little heat, but after this period heat will be required to keep the greenhouse temperature between 40 to 50°F (4 to 10°C).

You will need to know how the various types of chrysanthemum that are offered can be identified from the nursery-man's catalogue. Cultivars that have been registered for exhibition will have a symbol after their name to indicate when they will bloom in a normal season and what type and colour they will be. For instance, all cultivars that flower between August and the end of September will have a prefix of a number between 20 and 30, cultivars that flower during October will have a prefix between 13 and 19 inclusive, while late cultivars will have prefixes from 1 to 12. The type of bloom is shown as follows:

- large exhibition are classified as 1
- medium exhibition are classified as 2
- incurve are classified as either 3, 13 or 23
- reflexed are classified as either 4, 14 or 24
- intermediate are classified as either 5, 15 or 25
- sprays are classified as either 9, 19 or 29

After the number a small letter, either a, b or c, is given.

- 'a' represents a large-flowered cultivar
- 'b' represents a medium-flowered cultivar
- 'c' represents a small-flowered cultivar

In the case of sprays:

- 'a' represents anemone-centred
- 'b' represents pompon
- 'c' represents reflex flowers
- 'd' represents single flowers
- 'e' represents intermediate (incurving types)
- 'f' represents spiders, quills, spoons and any other types

The large letter indicates the colour of the bloom, for example the letter P indicates pink, DP dark pink, and LP light pink. So if a cultivar is advertised as '"Ann Dickson" 25a LB' it would mean that the cultivar blooms between August and the end of September, that it is an intermediate form, large bloom and light bronze in colour. '"Linda Young" 15b LY' indicates that the cultivar will flower from early November onwards, is an intermediate of medium size, and is light yellow in colour.

OBTAINING RELIABLE STOCK

Plants can be obtained from many sources in early spring, including supermarkets, garden centres, professional nurserymen, shops, and personal friends. The majority of the plants sold by supermarkets and garden centres will have been raised by professional nurserymen who have supplied them in bulk. Although most plants are properly named, the attendants are often unable to give the customer any idea of the height, colour or type so it becomes a hit-and-miss affair which often results in the buyer growing plants that are either inappropriate for the chosen site (perhaps too tall), or are the wrong type of flower completely. The plants in these outlets may be cheaper, but there is always a risk that some have been bought in from a local grower who may have infected stock. I would therefore recommend buying from a specialised chrysanthemum nursery after making your selection from their catalogue. If in doubt, write and ask for their opinion on the selection you require, or if a friend is supplying the plants, see them growing and acquire plants you feel will suit your particular requirements.

Plants ordered from a nursery will be supplied at the time you specify, which will depend on the facilities you have available to protect the young plants before it is time to plant out. The plants can be supplied ready for planting out immediately, but bear in mind that they will be small, with very little root system, and will take longer to get established than plants which have been individually potted on from early deliveries. Therefore, if you have a cold greenhouse or a cold frame that can be kept free from frost, I would recommend asking for the plants to be delivered in mid-March to give them that little extra start before planting out.

Plants that are supplied direct from a specialised chrysanthemum nursery will have been grown from ones checked for diseases and viruses. The mother plants are usually kept in a section of the nursery known as the 'health unit' and are continually checked for any sign of deterioration in their normal characteristics. They are also subjected to regular inspection by an official of the Ministry of Agriculture, Fisheries and Food. The plants you receive will have been rooted in sterilised compost and be growing well.

A START FOR YOUR PLANTS

Basic Plant Foods

Success with all plants, providing they have sufficient light and water, is mainly due to the correct amount of nutrients available to the plant in the correct order at all stages of growth. The main ingredients are nitrogen, phosphorus and potassium, with smaller amounts of calcium, magnesium, sulphur, iron and manganese, and even smaller amounts of what are commonly called 'trace elements', such as boron, copper and zinc. These ingredients are mixed to the correct proportions in branded pre-packed composts. However, most garden soils contain nearly all the ingredients necessary to sustain growth and only need topping up from time to time to keep the soil in a balanced condition. It is when the nutrients become out of balance that problems commence; therefore, it is important that your plants are given the ideal environment from the beginning.

Compost

If the plants' delivery date is between mid-March and the end of April they will require potting on, either in individual 3½in (9cm) pots or in a tray containing eight to twelve plants. The ideal compost for this first potting is either John Innes No. 1 or a soilless seed compost. Plants potted on in a soilless compost will get away very much quicker than those in a loam-based compost, but will take longer to get established in the open ground, especially if your soil is of the heavy type.

For the first potting you should buy the compost, in which the loam and peat used will have been sterilised. It should be purchased well in advance of the expected arrival of the plants and stored in the greenhouse or garden shed. The pots or trays should be clean and ready for use. If, however, it is your intention to mix your own compost the ingredients necessary to promote active growth are given below.

Loam

This is the most important ingredient in the compost. It should be slightly greasy to the touch with a crumb structure containing plenty of fibre, and with a pH rating of 6.5. Beginners should purchase sterilised loam from either a garden centre or nursery, although it is possible to make your own (*see* pages 129–131).

Peat, Bark and Leaf Mould

Peats have been used as the basis of soilless compost over the last few years, and this has meant that they are becoming more costly all the time. As a result, experiments have been carried out to find a substitute, adding wood bark to composts instead of peat, or mixed with the peat. The results have been very encouraging. Unfortunately, leaf mould, derived from beech and oak leaves, is virtually impossible to obtain, and as a result most composts are made with either peat or wood bark.

If peat is to be used it should be a sedge peat, widely agreed to be the best for chrysanthemums, which can be obtained from any garden centre in small bales or packs. An increasing number of garden centres also carry a supply of wood bark.

Sharp Sand or Fine Grit

It is essential that the compost has good, open drainage to allow the roots to breathe and allow excessive moisture to escape. The sand used must therefore be of the sharp non-caking type with granules ranging from the very fine up to ⅛in (0.3cm) in diameter. Sand similar to that used in the manufacture of concrete is ideal.

John Innes Composts

The ideal potting compost for chrysanthemums is the well-known John Innes. Most gardeners will have heard of these composts, formulated by the John Innes Horticultural Institution, whose formulae over the years have given reliable results to both the exhibitor and the professional chrysanthemum grower. The measurements and weights given below should therefore be strictly adhered to.

Small quantities of compost can be mixed as follows: construct a box measuring 14×8×3in (35×20×7.5cm). This tray will be the standard unit of measurement for each ingredient to be used when filled level but not compacted.

Measure out:

7 trays of loam (passed through a 6mm riddle)
3 trays of damp peat
2 trays of coarse dry sand

This amount equals 2.49 cubic feet, or exactly two bushels, and to it should be added the fertiliser:

3oz (75g) hoof and horn
3oz (75g) superphosphate of lime
1oz (25g) sulphate of potash
1oz (25g) ground chalk or limestone

The mixture for John Innes composts Nos. 2, 3 and 4 has the same amount of loam, peat and sand as the No. 1 compost but the amount of fertiliser is doubled for No. 2, trebled for No. 3 and is four times the amount for No. 4 for each bushel.

The hoof and horn, superphosphate of lime, and sulphate of potash can be purchased as 'John Innes Base Fertiliser', already mixed to the correct proportions, from any garden centre. Therefore 7oz (175g) of this base fertiliser could be added to two bushels of mixed loam, peat and sand. The ground chalk or limestone will have to be purchased separately and added as the compost is being prepared.

The measurements in these composts refer to the bushel. There are 8 gallons (36 litres) to the bushel, so for a large volume of compost it would be better to measure the loam, peat and sand with a 2-gallon (9-litre) bucket at the same ratio as given for the seed tray, except that every four buckets of mixed ingredients will measure a bushel.

Young plants should not be planted directly into freshly-made compost as the chemicals could burn the tender young roots. It is better to mix the compost ten to fourteen days before it is required, and during that period turn the compost every two to three days to allow any gases to escape and the chemicals to become thoroughly mixed within the compost. The compost should be covered during this period to prevent it drying out, but not covered too tightly, otherwise the gases cannot escape.

The compost should not be too dry or too wet for potting. A good test is to pick up a handful of compost and squeeze it – when the hand is opened the compost should retain its shape, and when tapped it should fall apart.

FIRST POTTING

If the plants are ordered for delivery in March or early April they should be potted on as soon as they arrive into the correct compost, preferably a loam-based one for outdoor cultivars and either soilless or loam-based for late cultivars.

The 3½in (9cm) pots should be clean, and if they are clay should be soaked in water for 24 hours before use (so that they are fully charged with water), and then allowed to stand to drain off any excess water. This will prevent the pot extracting moisture from the compost and drying it out.

There is no need to put crock in the bottom of the pot at this stage, so place about 1in (2.5cm) of the new compost in the bottom of the pot and slightly firm it, then spread the roots of the plant in the centre of the pot on to the new compost and fill around the plant to within ½in (1cm) of the lip. Gently tap the sides of the pot to settle the new compost around the plant, and finally gently firm the top of the compost around the plant with the fingers. Give the plant an overhead spraying with water, and stand it in the cold frame.

GROUND PREPARATION

The ground chosen should be well drained with an open aspect, and, if the soil is of the heavy clay type, digging should be done in the early autumn whilst the ground is not too wet to work on, incorporating well-rotted farmyard manure, mushroom compost or garden compost. However, light sandy soils can be left until early spring. If the proposed area is a border or part of an existing planted area and not a permanent bed, then normal digging would be sufficient. If you intend to grow blooms for exhibition you should consider preparing a permanent bed at this stage, as time spent on this at the beginning will prove beneficial later.

If the area has been cultivated before, the chances are that the nutrients required for chrysanthemums will not be perfect, so your first job is to have the soil tested by a specialist company. The small cost of this service will save both time and money and will ensure that your efforts are not wasted. Samples should be taken from six different parts of the plot where the plants are to be grown, by removing the top 2 to 3in (5 to 7.5cm) of soil and then taking a trowel-full of soil from 3 to 8in (7.5 to 20cm) deep. Mix the six

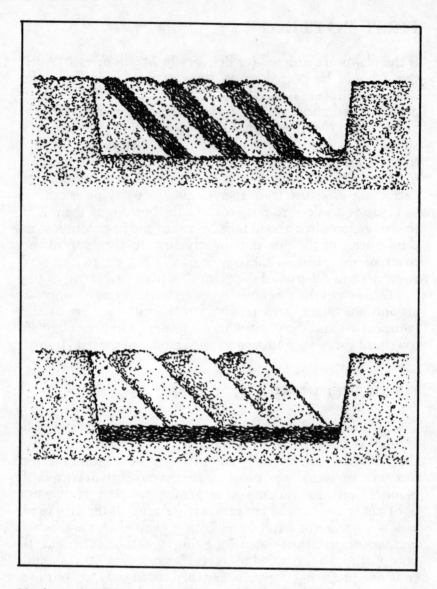

Newly turned over soil showing the position of the manure.

samples together, removing any stones and allow them to dry naturally for two or three days. Send a sample of the mixture (approximately 4oz/100g) in a plastic bag for analysis, stating that the area is to be used for chrysanthemums.

Whilst the results are being obtained, digging and incorporating farmyard manure can be done without affecting the main nutrient content of your soil. The farmyard manure will add valuable humus and trace elements to the soil.

Autumn Digging

The practice of double digging has been carried out for many years, but I am not convinced that it is beneficial if the ground is well drained and the top soil is less than 15in (37.5cm) deep. Sub soil has not been exposed to the elements for thousands of years, unlike the top soil, and consequently its make-up lacks the humus of rotting vegetation and animal manures which, combined with sediments, has produced the fertile top soil.

Excavate a trench 24in (60cm) wide the full width of the plot down to a depth of 12in (30cm), or to the sub soil, whichever is first, and barrow this soil to the end of the plot for use later. Then fork the bottom of the trench over to prevent compaction and turn over the next spit of soil into the trench.

Once the whole width has been turned, place a liberal dressing of manure at an angle against the newly-turned soil, if it is of the heavy clay type (not in the bottom of the trench, see diagram opposite). From my own experience I have found that wet, black farmyard manure placed in the bottom of a trench in heavy clay ground will be prevented from breaking down easily and could cause problems with drainage. In light sandy soils manure should be placed in the bottom of the trench, which will give the reverse effect, that of retaining moisture, and will break down readily. At this stage no fertilisers should be added.

This method of digging should be carried out throughout the whole plot. The area should be left and large lumps of soil should remain exposed for the winter frosts to break down.

Spring Digging

The method of preparation is exactly the same for light and heavy soils as described for autumn digging, but when the area is completed it should be raked level and the large lumps of earth broken down into fine particles to receive the plants.

Once the whole area has been prepared and the soil is of a fine tilth, marking out the beds should be considered, bearing in mind that if the plants are to be planted in rows then the taller plants should be placed at the back or in the middle row. The ideal size of bed would be around 4ft (1.2m) wide; this would allow three rows of plants – one row 6in (15cm) in from the edge, the second row 2ft (60cm) in and the third 3ft 3in (1m). This would allow access to the middle row of plants from both sides.

Three to four weeks before planting out the fertiliser should be applied to the top 3 to 4in (7.5 to 10cm) of soil (applying the amount of fertiliser as advised by the soil testing company) and thoroughly worked in. A word of warning – never give more than the recommended amount. Applying the fertiliser in advance of planting out ensures that it will be broken down and readily available to the plant. If no soil analysis has been done, then a well-balanced chrysan-themum fertiliser, applied at the rate of 3 to 4oz (75 to 100g) per square yard (metre), should be used. A weekly raking of the plot will keep it free from weeds and ensure the fertiliser is thoroughly mixed into the top layer of soil, ready to receive the plants.

EARLY-FLOWERING PLANTS

Plants that have been received early and potted on should be moved into a cold frame by mid-March, but they will still require protection from frost. Covers should be left on during the first two weeks and extra covers such as old sacks or carpet kept handy to put over the cold frame at night if there is a possibility of frost.

Watering should be kept to a minimum after the plants have become established in their pots. It should preferably be carried out early in the morning to allow the plants to dry off before nightfall. Also, a regular spraying of insecticide should be given every ten days to keep the plants clean.

The aim, from this point in time, is gradually to harden off the young plants ready for planting out. The covers should be opened gradually, a little more each day, if the weather permits. Make sure that driving rain, which could leave them saturated throughout the night, cannot be blown on to the plants. Towards the latter part of April the plants should be sufficiently hardy for the covers to be removed, but replace them if a severe frost is forecast.

During the period the plants are in the cold frame some cultivars will have grown tall (especially if they have been given plenty of water) and they will require supporting with a 2ft (60cm) split cane. The cane should be cut so that it is not too long and does not come in contact with the underside of

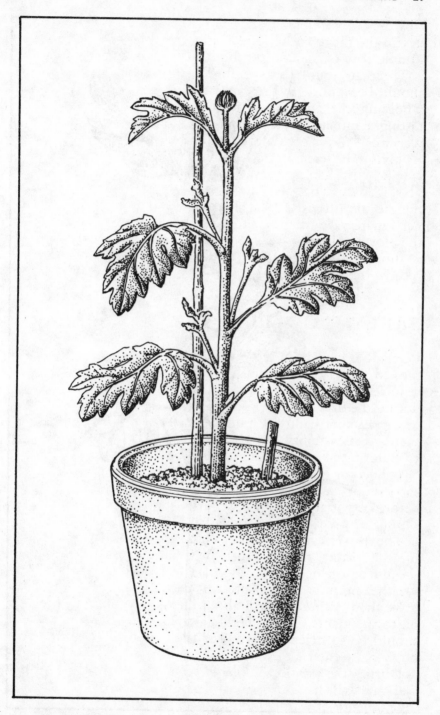

The plant before the growing point has been removed
(stopped).

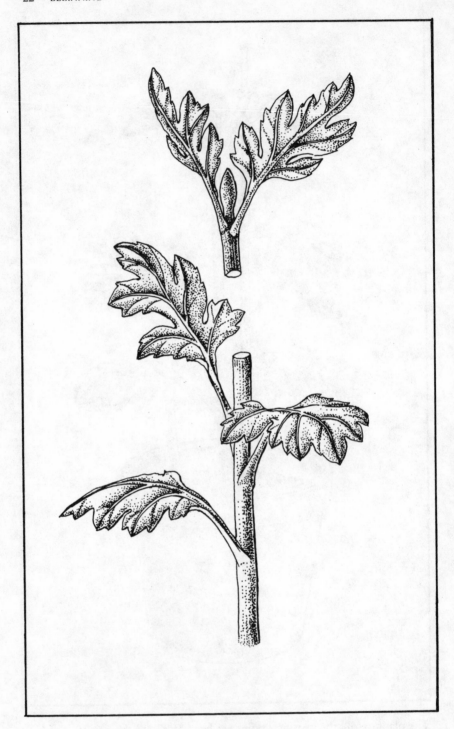

The plant after stopping.

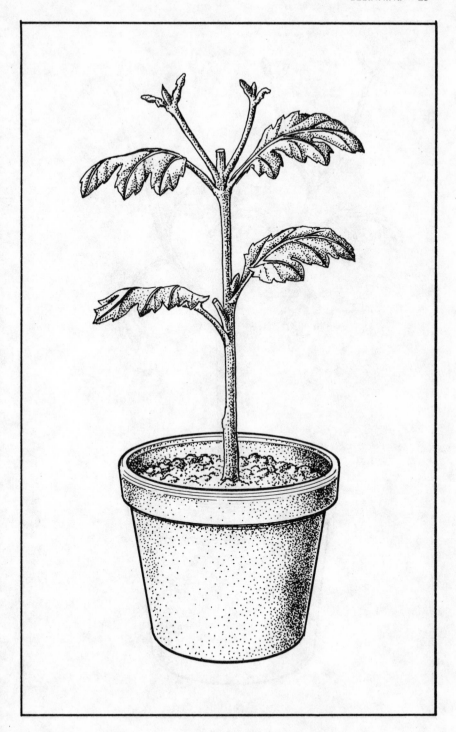

A plant showing laterals growing after first stop.

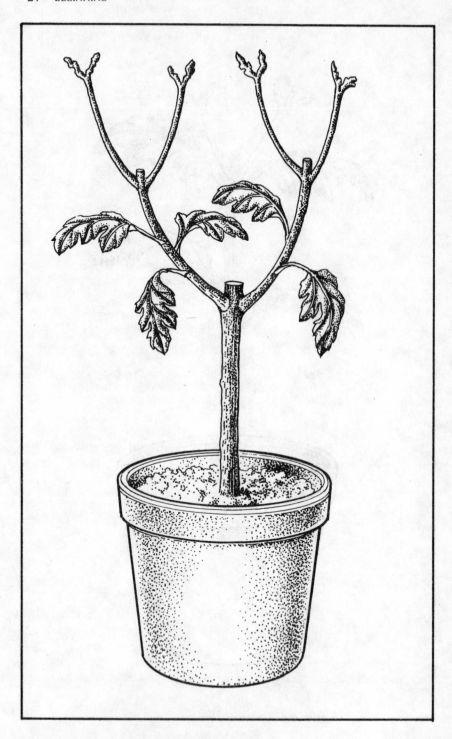

A plant showing laterals growing after second stop.

the covers. Insert the cane about 1in (2.5cm) from the main stem of the plant, which is then loosely secured to the cane, making sure that the stem growth is not restricted.

Some cultivars that are being grown for exhibition may require an early stop during April, so check with the nurseryman's catalogue. If this is the case, remove the growing point from the plant, making sure that only the point is removed and that the leaves surrounding the growing tip are not damaged (*see* diagram on page 22).

Late flowering plants which have been potted on into 3½in (9cm) pots should be ready for the next move into 5in (12.5cm) pots in early April. If the roots are projecting through the drainage hole at the bottom, then the plant is ready for repotting. The plants should be given a good watering twenty-four hours before they are to be potted on, so that they are fully charged with moisture.

You should use John Innes No. 2 for this repotting, or one of the many soilless composts that are now available. If you are preparing the compost yourself it should have been made ready at least two weeks before it is required, and should not be too wet, but just sufficiently so to hold together when squeezed in the hand. If traditional clay pots are to be used, remember to soak them before use. Plastic pots will not require this treatment but nevertheless should be clean.

The drainage holes at the bottom of the pot will require covering; this is best done by placing small pieces of broken pot around and over the hole, taking care not to seal the hole. The idea is to prevent the soil from falling out and to allow excess water to escape. Place a covering of approximately 1in (2.5cm) of the new compost over the crock in the bottom of the pot and firm slightly with a rammer (a piece of wood about 1in/2.5cm square is ideal), then gently knock the plant out of the small pot and stand in the centre of the new compost in the larger pot. Gently fill around the plant with the new compost up to the top of the soil on the plant. Tap the side of the pot so that the compost compacts around the plant, and it can then be firmed with the fingers and topped up to the same level as the original soil on the plant. This should leave almost 1in (2.5cm) from the top edge of the pot to the soil level for watering. If the plant requires a support use a small split cane, but be sure not to tie the stem of the plant too tightly; just a loose loop is sufficient to allow for development.

If soilless compost is used there is no need to cover the

drainage holes of the pot with crock. The first 1in (2.5cm) of compost will only require slight compression, then you should continue as above. Make sure that the label naming the cultivar is placed back into the pot after potting. This is a simple, obvious point, but one we all forget once in a while!

2

Outdoor Chrysanthemums

EARLY-FLOWERING CULTIVARS

Planting Out

The actual date for transplanting young plants from their pots or trays into their permanent position in the garden depends on the weather. There is no point in rushing to plant out if conditions are not favourable, since this will only retard plant development and all the hard work of protecting the young plants could be wasted. In southern England the last week in April is usually regarded as the safe time whereas in the north of Britain it could be as late as the third week in May. Although frosts have been known in late May the plants should be hard enough to stand up to a mild frost if they are prepared properly.

In southern counties of Britain the cold frame covers should have been gradually opened from early April and totally removed by the third week, allowing the plants to become acclimatised to night temperatures. In the north, opening the frames may not be started until the middle or even the third week of April. If there is a cold spell forecast, the covers should be replaced.

Two or three days before planting out, place the plants in groups out on the open ground near to the area where they are to be planted. This allows them to get acclimatised. Give the plants a good watering the day before you actually start planting out, making sure that each plant is thoroughly soaked. This watering is best done in the morning to allow any surplus to drain off before nightfall.

The plants that are to be planted individually amongst other flowering plants for garden decoration and the occasional cut blooms will need to have some form of support. I would recommend four canes set in the form of a square and slightly at an angle, not vertical, so that as the plant grows the laterals can be supported by running strings or garden twine around the cane.

Border Chrysanthemums

Small, compact varieties such as *Frutescens*, cushions, and early-flowering charms grow to a height of 10 to 14in (25 to 35cm), producing a delightful display of flowers in a wide range of colours, ideal for the border.

Chrysanthemums for Cutting or Garden Decoration

If the plants are to be grown in groups for cut blooms I would suggest that they are of the same cultivar, or of similar height, and are set out either as single rows supported by canes or grown in groups of twelve through 5in (12.5cm) square mesh netting, made of either mild wire or nylon. The netting is cut to the required size and placed on the ground, and a sturdy post is knocked into each of the corner squares, at a slight outward-leaning angle. The plants are then planted in the spaces. A good guide for setting the plants apart is to plant spray-type cultivars in every other square or disbud types in every third square. As the plants develop the netting is lifted up the posts to support them.

Extra care will be needed to prevent damaging the roots when removing the plants from the trays or pots. In the case of pots, providing the plants were watered the day before they should slip out easily. The left hand is placed over the top of the pot with the stem of the plant passing between the middle finger and the forefinger, then turned upside down and given a sharp tap on the bottom. In the case of trays I have found that it is better to lift a single plant from the corner of the tray, then gradually work the hand under the other plants' root system. Lift the whole tray full of plants out in one go and carefully pull them apart. Some damage to the roots will occur, but not as much as if each individual plant was dissected from the other in the tray.

Chrysanthemums for Exhibition

Cultivars that are to be grown for exhibition will require a little more consideration at planting out time, because at a later stage of development these blooms will require protection from the weather. Therefore, depending on the type of cultivar chosen, you may need overhead covers, which should be put up prior to planting out. There are various forms of cover, but if your intention is to become an exhibitor, you should think seriously about both the type of material to be used and its construction. *See* page 61 for more details.

Reflexed Cultivars

Normally reflexed cultivars grown under cover produce better blooms than those protected by paper bags, but some top exhibitors have had good results with reflexes grown in a wire frame cover, which supports a large paper or special plastic bag, attached to the plant. It is therefore better to group all the reflexed cultivars together in one bed so that they can be covered; this reduces the area to be covered and therefore the expense.

Intermediate and Incurve Cultivars

Exhibition blooms of these cultivars can be grown success-fully protected by double greaseproof paper bags and grown in the open ground without overhead protection, or with a single greaseproof bag if grown under covers.

Spray Cultivars

Most spray cultivars can be successfully grown without any protection at all but singles and anemone cultivars are better grown under covers.

PLANT SUPPORTS

Supporting cultivars, in particular exhibition ones, is very important, as each stem will need to be held up individually, regardless of whether it carries one or a number of blooms (as in the case of spray types). Therefore, many top exhibitors usually use one cane to support each lateral stem.

If canes are to be used always select one at least 12in (30cm) longer than the expected height of the plant. This will leave enough to allow the cane to be pushed well into the ground. The cane should also be long enough to support

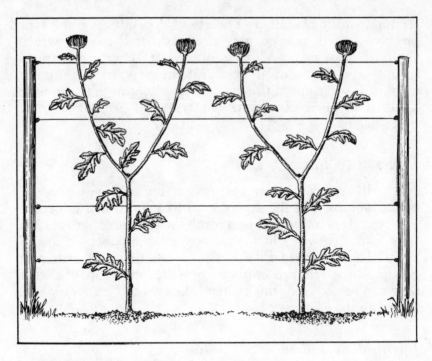

Cordon system of support showing supporting lines.

the plant without rubbing the developing bloom, although it can always be pushed down a little more if necessary.

One good method is the cordon system which consists of metal posts 6 to 7ft (2–2.1m) long, set out in a straight line with intermediate posts every 8ft (2.4m). Nylon baling twine is then run and secured to each post in the line some 6in (15cm) above ground level, then every 6in (15cm) up the posts to a height of 3ft (90cm). One line is then placed 9in (22.5cm) above this. Complete every inside row up to this stage before you start planting, as this prevents the twine becoming tangled up with newly-planted chrysanthemums. Then start planting your centre rows first, bearing in mind that these must hold the tallest cultivars. Secure each plant stem to the horizontal twine line with a special clip in the shape of a W (*see* diagram opposite). The distance between plants should be 18 to 24in (45 to 60cm), depending on the amount of space available.

Once the row has been planted, start running the horizontal lines on the outside row. Only two lines are erected at this stage, again starting 6in (15cm) above the ground (additional lines can be secured as the plants develop). Plant the outside

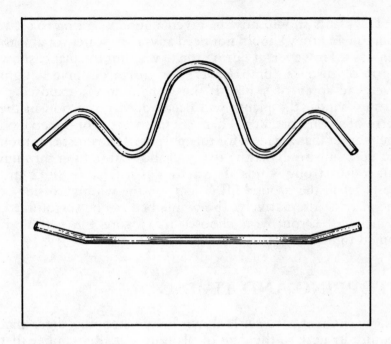

'W' supporting clip.

rows, setting the plants out so that each is midway between those in the centre row. This gives a staggered pattern, which will allow each plant to get the maximum light. Each plant should then be secured as before.

This method of support has proved to be very effective even in high winds, as the whole row of plants sways together at the same rate, thus preventing damage from the blooms beating against each other. Providing that the string lines are kept tight at all times and the heads of the flowers are supported by a string line just below the base of the bloom, most blooms will come to no harm. Cultivars with thin necks will require a split cane secured to the neck as the bloom develops, but up to bud-bagging stage no additional support will be necessary.

It is better to complete the planting out of each batch of cultivars as you progress and put a label at the beginning of each different cultivar, because after they are planted you will have difficulty in identifying where each starts and ends. You can mark the rows with the name of the cultivar, and in addition make a plan showing exactly where each cultivar has been planted. This also gives you vital information for future planning and records.

The plants should now be given a good watering to settle them in and they should not need any more water for at least ten days. However, if during the day any of the plants show signs of distress (limp leaves, for instance), give a light overhead spray of water. If the planted area is exposed to strong winds, the plants will need added protection in the form of a wind breaker. There are many types of material on the market that are ideal for this purpose. The most common is a very fine mesh netting that will allow air to filter through but resists strong winds. The netting is secured to 8ft (2.4m) posts set in the ground 2ft (60cm) on the windward side of the plants. Alternatively, the whole bed can be surrounded. Whichever layout you choose, make sure the netting is pulled tight.

STOPPING AND TIMING

Allow the plants to settle down before stopping those that require it, near to the date of planting out. Remember that stopping dates are only an approximation based on results obtained from records kept during the growing season. As climatic conditions can alter the actual flowering date by as much as ten days, it is useful to allow for this when stopping plants for show. If a stopping date is known, it is advisable to stop half the plants about seven days before and the remainder as given – this would improve your chances of having blooms for the show. Nurserymen's catalogues usually give the stopping dates for new cultivars that they are releasing based on the plant's performance at their nursery. Therefore, if the plants were purchased from a nursery in the northern part of Britain an adjustment would have to be made if the plants were to be grown in the south. For example, the stopping date given for 'Peter Rowe' in northern Britain is 25 April, and in the south is 25 May. The dates given may or may not give you the blooms on the required day, so it is important to list everything you do, as this will be the basis for future cultivation and success.

Plants that are to be grown for cut flowers or for garden display can be stopped at any time up to the beginning of June. It is better to stop two or three plants on the same day and then another two or three plants a week later, as this will give a succession of blooms. Spray cultivars that are to be grown for show should all be stopped by June and in some cases before this date; the nurseryman will be able to advise on a suitable date for each cultivar. Cultivars that have been stopped in early April should now be showing signs of laterals growing from the leaf axil. Be careful not to damage these tender young shoots when securing the plant to either the string line or to the cane as these are the potential exhibition flower stems.

Once the plants have become established it is time to consider a spraying routine to deal with the common garden pests. The aim is to *prevent* an infestation, not wait until you have to eliminate one, so the first spraying should be given during the first week of planting out and then at regular ten day intervals. A good practice is to alternate pesticides in order to minimise the chances of the pest becoming immune to one particular insecticide. The following method has proved successful in combating most common pests. The first spraying consists of Sybol 2 mixed with Nimrod T as recommended in the manufacturers' instructions. This spray will have a double action, as an insecticide to deal with greenfly and as a fungicide to prevent mildew. The second spraying would be of Tumblebug, the third spraying would be Nico-Soap, and then the first spraying is repeated, as above, and so on.

LATE-FLOWERING CULTIVARS

During April the plants in the 5in (12.5cm) pots should be gradually hardened off by removing the frame covers, and the final pots made ready for use. The compost should be either mixed ten to fourteen days in advance or purchased from the local garden centre or nurseryman.

If a loam-based compost is to be used it should be equivalent to John Innes No. 3 or No. 4 for this final potting (most top exhibitors tend to prefer a mixture to the strength of John Innes No. 4). There are two basic differences between this mix and the previous ones: they contain a greater amount of fertiliser, and the loam should not be riddled but chopped into small lumps about 1in (2.5cm) in diameter. The rest of the ingredients are the same and in the same proportions. Remember to turn the heap of mixed compost every other day before use.

If the final potting is to be in a soilless bought compost, or a soilless compost mixed yourself, the ingredients are 75 per cent sphagnum peat and 25 per cent fine sand or grit. Added to a bushel of this mix is a recommended amount of Chempak Mix fertiliser. Care in mixing is of the utmost importance so that all the chemical fertilisers are equally dispersed throughout the compost, otherwise the tender young roots could be burned.

During the latter part of April the standing ground should be prepared where the late flowering plants will be grown during the summer season. A little care in choosing the site will pay dividends later. If possible, try to select a position that is open to all-round sunshine so that the rows run from north to south. This will give each row of plants the opportunity to enjoy the sunshine from both sides.

Mark out each row by knocking in a strong post at each end and intermediate posts every 10ft (3m), with the distance between each row not less than 3ft (90cm). The posts need to be about 6ft (1.8m) long and should be driven firmly into the ground. Attach either baling twine or wire to the posts about 4ft (120cm) above the ground, making sure that it is pulled tight. The pots should not stand directly on the soil as earth worms can get in through the drainage holes, thus allowing water and liquid feed to escape before the plant has had time to take advantage of it. Also in very wet weather the pot can become waterlogged which could cause the plant to die. The best method is to stand the pots either on a board or bricks. Try an open type standing board, consisting of two strips of timber nailed to short lengths of 2×2in (5×5cm) timber, with gaps between to allow free drainage from the hole in the pot.

Having set out each row, it is now possible to calculate how many plants the area will accommodate without over-crowding. The minimum distance between pots should not be less than 4in (10cm). Once you have prepared the site, the job of final potting can begin.

Final Potting

The plants should be given a good watering the day before potting, and the final pots should be immersed in a tub of clean water for twenty-four hours prior to being used.

Before potting it is best to place all cultivars in groups so that each plant can be checked over against plants of the same variety, and the final selection of the number of plants to be grown can be made. The selected plants should be as far as possible at the same stage of development, and inferior plants should be discarded.

A good supply of washed crock (clean broken clay pot pieces) will be required, together with a ball of string or raffia, canes in varying lengths, a small rammer made from a 1in (2.5cm) square piece of wood about 15in (37.5cm) long, a selection of large pots (varying from 8 to 10 inches/20–25cm), and a small shovel or trowel. It is an advantage to find out from members of a local society or the nurseryman the size of pots that should be used for the cultivars that are to be grown. A general guide is as follows:

- Large, medium exhibition and large singles – 9–10in (22.5–25cm) pots
- Incurve, reflexed, intermediate and medium singles – 8–9in (20–22.5cm) pots
- Late sprays planted singly – 5in (12.5cm) pots; group of three – 9in (22.5cm) pot
- Charms and cascades – 7–9in (17.5–22.5cm) pots

At this stage it is better to have an extra pot of each variety, providing sufficient standing room is available, but do not overcrowd the plants. Grow a few plants well, rather than having too many that will be a waste of time and space.

Check the compost to make sure it is in the right condition – just sufficiently moist to hold together when squeezed in the hand. If it is too dry, give it a little light watering, mix well and delay the potting until the next day. If it has become too wet, spread it out and allow it to dry out partially. Select canes (slightly shorter than the expected height to which the plant will grow) and then potting can begin.

Place a large portion of crock over the drainage hole in the base of the pot and then smaller pieces over and around. Take a small shovel or trowel full of the rougher compost from around the base of the compost heap, and place this over the crock in the bottom of the pot, to a depth of 1in (2.5cm). (Many top exhibitors place a layer of either well-rotted manure or peat in the bottom of the pot first, and then a thin layer of compost on top to allow a little more moisture retention.) Gently firm the compost by ramming. Place your hand over the top of the 5in (12.5cm) pot so that the stem passes between the middle fingers, turn the pot upside down and remove it. If the pot does not lift off, gently tap the rim to release the plant. Carefully remove the crock from the rootball of the plant and then insert the plant in the centre of the large pot, so that its base is resting firmly on the new compost; add compost around the plant until the pot is filled, gently tapping the side of the pot. When the new compost around the plant roots has reached the level of the top of the old compost, it should be gently rammed. As the compost is compressed, additional compost is added until the new compost is level with the surface of the old. The surface level should finish approximately 2in (5cm) below the rim of the pot, to allow for watering and, at a later date, top dressing.

Many exhibitors ram the new compost very hard around the plant on cultivars such as incurves, and only lightly around reflex varieties, but this will depend on the type of loam being used. For example, a very heavy loam should only be gently rammed, whilst a sandy type loam will need heavier ramming. Soilless composts should only be firmed with the fingers.

As each pot is completed, insert the label and then the canes into the new compost, making sure that the canes do not damage the roots. The number of canes each plant will require varies. Large and medium exhibition need only one cane, while large reflexes or intermediates need two, medium reflexes and incurves three, and singles four. When securing the plant to the canes it is better to use raffia or some other type of material that will not chafe the stem of the young plant. The raffia should be tied around the stem of the plant in a loose loop to allow the stem to develop and then secured to the canes. If the plant has been stopped and laterals are already growing, the first tie should be below the laterals and a second tie should be made incorporating the growing laterals. As each batch of cultivars is completed, the pots should be grouped together, touching each other and given a light watering to settle them in. Leave them in that position for a day or so.

When transferring the plants to the final standing ground, select cultivars of the same height for each row, to prevent tall cultivars from over-shadowing shorter ones. Secure each cane to the horizontal wire or twine with a metal clip (see page 31).

The plants should now be sprayed, as described for early cultivars.

3

Securing, Disbudding and Feeding

From this period on the emphasis must be to encourage active root growth into the surrounding soil, so water should be withheld unless the plants start to show signs of distress. Always check the plants in the morning to see if they have recovered from flagging from the previous day and, if they have, withhold water. Too much water at this stage will not encourage the roots to develop and this will result in poor quality blooms later. This applies equally to exhibition blooms and cut flowers. No matter how much feed is applied during the growing season, the end results are determined by the activity of the roots and this is therefore one of the most important factors to success.

Cleanliness around the plants will help to eliminate some of the hiding places of the pests that are closely allied to the chrysanthemum, so removing weeds, dead leaves, and so on, will decrease the chances of infection. Hoeing between and around the plants should be a routine job during the first early weeks after planting, but later, when the feeding roots come much nearer to the surface, this job will have to be done by hand. Canes that are used to support laterals are the ideal hiding places for earwigs which will make their home in the hollow section at the top, so seal the top of the cane with putty.

Birds have been known to remove the young growing points of plants that have been stopped, giving the plants a second stop, which could be disastrous to the exhibitor. Some form of bird scarer would be advisable.

Slugs love young growing plants and an effective method of eradication should be put into operation as soon as the plants are planted out. If slug bait is used, be sure that the bait is only available to the slugs and not to birds and animals. A simple and safe method of trapping slugs is to set a shallow dish at ground level filled with beer.

The aim for exhibition blooms is to grow a well-balanced

plant, not too ripe and not too soft. Having encouraged a good root system, your thoughts should now turn to the development of the lateral, and the bud. The number of laterals allowed to develop will play an important part in the size of the finished blooms; the greater the number the smaller the blooms. For cut-flower purposes it will depend on individual preference, but for the exhibitor it becomes more critical. The refinement and form of a bloom is far more important to the exhibitor than size, so the exhibitor's target should be to obtain maximum size without losing either refinement or form. As a general guide, medium cultivars are grown three blooms per plant, whilst large cultivars are limited to two.

LATERALS AND BUD INITIATION

Plants that were stopped either just before or just after planting out will need a boost in the form of a high nitrogen feed three weeks after planting out. This will encourage lateral growth, and will also be of benefit to the plants that were stopped before because those plants will now be approaching the bud initiation stage of development. This is the moment when the growing point begins to form a bud, although it is invisible to the naked eye for a further four to five weeks. The feed should be a quick-acting type, either in powder form or liquid. If the feeding time coincides with a wet period, a dry feed in powder form should be used (perhaps ammonium nitrate applied at ½oz per square yard, raked into the top 2in (5cm) of soil. However, if the weather has been dry, a liquid feed should be used with ingredients such as NPK 25–0–10, or a stock solution can be made by mixing 7oz (175g) of potassium nitrate with 20oz (500g) of ammonium nitrate dissolved in one gallon (4.5 litres) of water. This stock solution is then diluted at the ratio of one part to two hundred parts water and each plant is given a pint (0.5 litre) of the diluted solution, with a second feed 10 days later.

CHRYSANTHEMUMS FOR CUTTING AND GARDEN DECORATION

If the aim is to have a display of small blooms, allow all the laterals to develop on both disbuds and spray cultivars. However, the size and quality of the blooms can be improved by reducing the number of laterals to four or five. As the laterals start to develop, all unwanted laterals should be removed when they are approximately 1in (2.5cm) long, but basal growth can either be left to produce a second crop of small blooms or cut off at ground level with a sharp knife. Cut them off rather than breaking them, because it is from this basal growth that you can take the cuttings to produce next year's plants, and you must avoid damaging the root system.

BORDER CHRYSANTHEMUMS

Early-Flowering Charms

These are similar to the late-flowering charms but flower from August through to October. They come in a wide range of colours, produce hundreds of small single blooms and vary in height from 10–18in (25–45cm). They are also suitable for tub decoration on a patio.

Frutescens Chrysanthemums

These are a type of ground-covering plant with fern-like foliage. The flowers range from single to anemone-type centres, and come in various colours, flowering at a height of 15in (37.5cm). The blooms are ideal for floral art work.

Cushion Chrysanthemums

These are a relatively new introduction to Britain. The plants can be grown as pot plants and flowered in the home. Once the plant has finished flowering it can be transferred to the border in October, and, providing it is covered with a little straw or peat during the winter, it will start growing in the spring to give a beautiful display of small blooms from July onwards. The blooms range from singles to doubles in all colours and grow to a height of 10in (25cm).

Exhibition Blooms

With exhibition cultivars it is always better to select laterals that are near to the top of the plant, similar in size and at the same stage of development. Always carry one extra lateral until the buds have been secured and tied in, then the extra one can be removed. Never select a vigorous lateral if it does not match the others. By carefully choosing laterals that are at the same stage of development you will increase the chance of more blooms to select at show time. All unwanted laterals should be removed and all basal growth cut off.

From early June the whole plant will start to develop rapidly and a good sign is the gradual increase in thickness of the laterals and size of the leaves. At this point a supplement feeding programme can be introduced, but it must be in the ratio of NPK 10–0–10. The principle is to keep the plant moving but also to ripen the laterals. Too much nitrogen would produce soft vegetative growth, and too much potash would produce hard stems which would restrict the flow of nutrients to the developing bud. Once the buds are visible and large enough to secure, select laterals of equal length with buds that are compatible to each other, and then remove the extra one which has been carried on by cutting it off as near to the leaf joint as possible. Many growers suggest that this spare lateral should be removed a little at a time, say, every other day, but it is perhaps better for the plant for it to be removed in one go as the healing process can then begin at once without being prolonged over a period of days.

BUDS AND THEIR SECURING

The buds will have started to develop some five to six weeks before they are ready for securing, by the cells of a single petal splitting to form two petals and those two petals in turn splitting and multiplying. It is now that an extra nitrogen feed is essential to speed up the multiplication and thus increase the number of petals the bloom will hold. It is too late once the bud has become visible, since the petal count has already been determined and therefore the overall size of the bloom is greatly influenced.

Securing Disbudded Cultivars for Exhibition

The securing of the buds for exhibition blooms is a delicate task and should be carried out with the utmost care. Remember that each plant has been reduced to the correct number of blooms it is to carry, and any mistake now cannot be rectified. For this reason, you should not be in too much of a hurry to secure a minute bud (with the exception of 'Venice' and its sports). Always allow the buds to develop around the crown bud on small stems about ¼in (0.5cm) long, before removing them, making sure not to damage the stem of the crown bud. Also secure batches of buds of the same cultivar at the same time and never at different times (this will give a better chance of blooms maturing together).

The moment the tiny buds are seen, the feeding programme should be changed to one of slightly higher nitrogen in relation to potassium. I have used the ratio NPK 30–0–20 in liquid form for many years, and give each plant 1 pint (0.5 litre) diluted to half strength on the first application (1–200), then the same ten days later at full strength (1–100). All further feeds are then given at half strength, until the calyx breaks, revealing the colour. At this point all feeding is stopped – if high nitrogen is given once the colour is showing, there is every possibility that the bloom will rot as it matures. This method of feeding, from securing the bud up to the colour show, is designed to encourage the tiny petals to grow to their maximum length and breadth.

The most important ingredient from the time the bud is seen is water. The plants should always be kept moist, and plants grown under cover should be watered every morning with approximately 4 pints (2 litres) of water per plant. Plants grown in the open ground are also kept moist at all times, watered as necessary and at any time during the day. Cultivars grown under cover are watered in the morning because they are mainly reflexed and therefore not bagged, so any surplus water needs sufficient time to evaporate before nightfall. This reduces the amount of moisture circulated in the air around the blooms at night when the temperatures are falling.

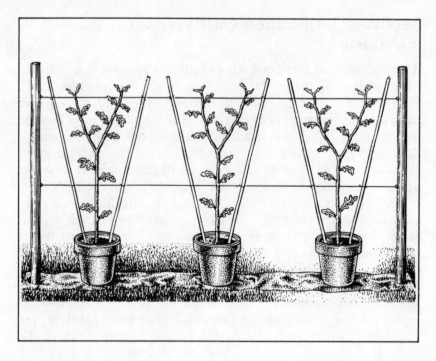

Supporting lines for pot plants.

Securing for Cut Flowers or Garden Decoration

Cultivars grown for cut blooms or garden decoration can be treated exactly as for exhibition blooms, except that more laterals are allowed to develop and flower. Securing each bud is exactly as described on page 41, with the exception of spray cultivars.

It is not necessary to feed to the same degree as on page 41. A general top dressing of a balanced chrysanthemum fertiliser at the rate of 1oz (25 g) per square yard, worked into the top soil around the plants in mid-June will provide sufficient food to give excellent results.

EARLY-FLOWERING SPRAYS

Cultivars that are to be grown for exhibition purposes will require a little more attention than those for garden decoration and cutting. The stopping dates of each cultivar will have to be decided on to obtain blooms for shows from early

September onwards. As a general rule, spray cultivars fall into two categories: those that flower from early August to mid-September (such as 'Madeleine', 'Red Wendy' and 'Broadway Mandy'), and the 'Margaret' family that flower from early September onwards. Stopping dates for the latter cultivars will be around 15 May in the north of Britain and 1 June in the south. For the earlier ones it will be around 1 June in the north of Britain and 15 June in the south. In some cases it is preferable to cut back the early type and grow on the basal shoots for show.

Again, a high nitrogen feed should be given, as described for exhibition blooms, to encourage the laterals to develop. Three to four weeks after stopping, the laterals will be growing well and now is the time to reduce the crop for exhibition to four laterals – select the best four laterals available. For general cut flowers and garden decoration let all the laterals develop to produce a mass of blooms.

Each lateral for exhibition will need to be supported individually as it develops, and a cane should be set in the ground at such angle that the bloom heads will be kept clear of each other. For cut flowers or garden decoration a cane placed on either side of the plant, and string or twine passed round the plant and secured to the canes, are sufficient. If your plants are growing in square mesh netting, just lift this as the laterals develop.

Securing Sprays for Exhibition

As the laterals approach the final phase of development to form the flower heads, the exhibitor must decide which type of spray he needs in order to comply with the show schedule. This may ask for either 'compound' or 'terminal' sprays.

On a compound spray, every bud on sub pedicels from the main pedicel is allowed to develop. With terminal sprays, only one bloom per main pedicel is allowed to develop, and all sub pedicels are removed (*see* diagram overleaf).

Most schedules have classes for both types of spray, but the terminal spray is the one that is mostly shown at top-quality exhibitions. Selection of the buds that are to produce the flowering head of the terminal spray is crucial. The aim is to have the maximum number of blooms of the same size at the same stage of development at the same time.

The first task is to remove the crown bud, known as the

(Left) Compound spray showing each bud on sub-pedicels to develop. (Right) Terminal spray showing one bloom on each main pedicel.

'apical bud', when this is large enough to handle without damaging the remaining buds. Leave the plant for two or three days so that the pedicels of the other buds develop a little more, then select the best five or six buds at the same stage of development down the stem, and remove all the rest (*see* diagram above). As the buds develop it will be necessary to remove any vegetative or bud growth that develops in the leaf axils. Once the buds are secured, a final high nitrogen liquid feed can be given, at full strength of 1 to 100, and at the rate of 1 pint (0.5 litre) per plant.

Many top exhibitors place short lengths of wire between the pedicels to keep the blooms apart during the first few days of development; these are removed once the pedicel has become ripe. This has a dual effect on the final head of blooms; they are positioned to give an overall pleasing effect, and they are not as easily damaged by the wind.

Hardy Garden Type Spray

In addition to the ordinary garden type spray there is a new introduction which is weather-proof and does not have to be dug up and stored over winter. All the gardener has to do is cut down the plant after flowering, and cover it with a suitable mulch. These hardy types are treated in exactly the same way as ordinary garden sprays, and come in various colours in single and double blooms. They grow to a height of 36in (90cm) and the range of types and colours make this new introduction ideal for flower arranging.

4

Late-Flowering Cultivars

WATERING

For plants being grown in pots, one way of checking whether or not they need watering is to tap the outside of the pot with a small wooden mallet. If the pot rings, then that plant requires watering – water *only* those plants that need it. The method of watering pot plants is very important – they should never be allowed to dry out completely (regardless of whether they are grown in a loam or soilless compost), but neither should they become waterlogged. If you adhere to the following guidelines, your plants will develop a strong root growth.

Each individual pot should be treated separately. If watering is to be done with a hose-pipe it is preferable to direct the flow of water on to a piece of broken pot laid on the top of the compost; this will prevent the water removing the compost and exposing the roots. A plant which requires watering should be given a good drink, by filling the pot to the rim, and not just a sip. Should the plant have become too dry, the compost may have shrunk away from the sides of the pot (when water is given it will escape at a great speed), and that plant will need more than one application of water to ensure that the compost expands to refill the pot.

Providing the compost has the right texture, water given should just soak through gently. Some exhibitors say they like the water to take three to four minutes to disappear from the surface, but as long as the water gently seeps away you know your compost is all right.

LATERALS FOR EXHIBITION

Some cultivars will have been stopped in either April or May, depending on whether they needed two stops or an early stop, and the laterals will need tying in every 6in (15cm) as they develop. Most cultivars stopped in April, such as incurves and singles, will require the second stop in early June. Late May up to the middle of June is the time when most of the decoratives (which include intermediate and reflex forms) are stopped.

When stopping cultivars such as singles and incurves for the second time, select three laterals which are as near identical as possible, remove the growing point from each and then remove the unwanted laterals. In the case of cultivars such as reflexes and intermediates that were stopped earlier, allow to develop three laterals on all the large types and four on mediums. Always select identical laterals. Never remove any spare laterals until the ones that you have selected have been supported, either by tying each lateral to a supporting cane or by looping a length of twine around both cane and laterals.

With large and medium exhibition cultivars you should allow three laterals to develop, but in this case select the laterals which are most vigorous and remove the rest.

CUT FLOWERS

Plants that are grown purely for cutting should be given one stop about mid-June and then as many breaks as required should be allowed to develop, bearing in mind that the larger your crop is, the smaller the blooms will be.

If the cultivars are of the December-flowering type, and the blooms are required for Christmas, the approximate stopping date is 25 July. Remember that they will require a heated greenhouse.

FEEDING

As with the early cultivars, the moment the plant has been stopped a high nitrogen feed at the rate of 1 pint (0.5 litre) per plant should be given to encourage the development of the new laterals.

The general feeding programme for pot plants should start approximately one month after final potting. There are various brands of solid fertiliser available, but be sure to select one that is balanced, containing nitrogen, phosphate, and potash in equal proportions. The recommended rate of one I have used for many years is a level teaspoonful every ten days, but I have found it better to give half the recommended rate every five days. The reason is that during the summer months the plants will need to be watered at least every other day, and possibly every day during a hot spell, so there is more chance of the nutrients being washed out of the pot. If the weather is very dry during June it is best to use a liquid feed at half strength every watering, but be sure that the compost is not dry or the plant foliage limp. If it is, water first and feed after. Liquid feed is usually purchased in crystal form and then diluted at a teaspoonful to 1 gallon (4.5 litres) of water for full strength – be guided by the manufacturer's recommendations. Even though the diluted solution looks weak, these are straight fertilisers and have been produced to give the best possible results at the recommended rates.

Buds will start to appear in the large and medium exhibition cultivars from early July onwards and from early August onwards in the others. The plants should never be allowed to dry out at this stage and from this period the compost should always be kept fully charged with water.

TOP DRESSING

During July, when the plant is approaching bud formation, a top dressing of compost similar to that used for final potting should be spread over the existing compost to a thickness of ½in (1cm). This will encourage more roots to form and keep the plant growing. It is usual to give the plants three top dressings during the season at monthly intervals.

BUD SECURING

Because of the limited number of plants grown, every precaution must be taken to ensure that each pot and lateral is secured firmly to its support. The plants can vary in height from 3 to 6ft (90 to 180cm) and are therefore vulnerable to high winds.

As the tiny buds appear, secure the crown bud (the 'apical bud'), by removing all the surrounding buds, taking care not to damage the stem of the crown bud. If the buds are too small, let them develop for a few more days before securing.

Having secured all the buds on the plant it should be left for a few days to allow the buds to develop, by which time each bud will give a clear indication as to whether the bud stem is worthy of final selection, or whether it has been damaged.

Because of climatic conditions some cultivars often produce buds too early for the required securing date, and hence too early for a particular show date. At this stage there are two ways to delay the flowering date by a few days:

(i) Do not secure the crown bud for another four to five days and let the secondary buds continue to grow during this period and then remove them. The blooms will be slightly smaller.

(ii) Remove the crown bud along with all except one of the small laterals which have developed around the crown bud. Allow this lateral to grow on and produce a flowering bud – this is commonly called a 'run on'. This will delay the flowering date in some cases for up to two weeks, but the disadvantage is that the height of the plant could increase by as much as 15in (37.5cm) on some cultivars.

Once the buds have been secured and given a few days to settle down, the next job is to select the number of laterals required on each cultivar. As a general guide, on incurved, reflexed and intermediate cultivars only two blooms are allowed to flower on large cultivars, and three on mediums. In the case of mediums in these sections, it is better to select laterals that are slightly thinner and of the same height, rather than three uneven laterals, although you may be tempted to retain two strong laterals.

On late-flowering singles, four or five blooms are normal on the large type, as many as ten blooms on mediums of the 'My Love' family, and six blooms on other medium singles. More blooms are allowed to develop on cultivars such as 'My Love' to reduce the number of rows of petals to as near to five as possible, and also to reduce the risk of petals growing from the flower disc.

Large exhibition cultivars (commonly called Japs) are grown one up, and the medium exhibition Japs are grown one or two up. With large exhibition cultivars it is best to select the bud that is sitting perfectly at right angles to the stem, and not one that is slightly tilted on the strongest break. Secure it to the cane before removing the remaining lateral. The same applies to medium exhibition cultivars, unless two blooms are required, in which case you should choose the best two and, as before, take off the remaining laterals.

FEEDING DURING BUD DEVELOPMENT

As with the early flowering cultivars, the feeding emphasis must be on keeping the plant in a balanced condition with a steady enlargement of both the stem and leaves up to the bud.

The most important ingredient from this stage on is water; the plants must never be allowed to flag and during hot sunny days an overhead spray will be beneficial.

Once the buds are secured, you should use a solid feed, with a slightly higher nitrogen content than potash content, at the rate of half a teaspoonful sprinkled on top of the compost and watered in every five days. Alternatively, you could try a liquid feed such as Chempak or Vitafeed, again at half the recommended rate every five days, until the calyx breaks and reveals the colour of the bloom.

Some cultivars do not like too much feed, and experience has shown that cultivars of the 'Fair Lady' family and medium singles do better from bud securing stage on half the rate given above – half a teaspoonful every ten days.

Once the calyx has broken, revealing the flower colour, you must protect those blooms intended for exhibition from both the weather and pests. Spray with Abol-G over and underneath the bud and then place a small greaseproof bag over the bud, securing it just below the bud with a bag-tie around the stem. This will provide ideal protection while you are preparing the greenhouse to receive the plants. Never be in too great a hurry to house the plants (unless weather conditions absolutely force you), as they will benefit more from open conditions.

HOUSING

The greenhouse should be completely tidied out and the glass cleaned on both sides. The inside of the greenhouse should be washed down with a disinfectant and any broken panes or leaks should be repaired. The windows should be sealed and the greenhouse fumigated with a sulphur candle. Leave the greenhouse sealed for ten to twelve hours before opening it up to full ventilation, and allow a further three to four hours before you start to work in the confines of the greenhouse. When the fumes have dispersed, erect light shading using muslin or some similar material to protect the blooms from excessive sunshine, as this could cause fading of the deep-coloured blooms. Check that the heating system and electric fans are in working order and ready for use.

When preparing to house the plants it is worth remembering that they are going into a restricted environment. Consideration should be given only to plants which are worthy of housing. The following tips have proved invaluable to me over the years.

(i)   Give all the plants a good watering and spray with a mixture of insecticide and fungicide the day before housing.

(ii)   Give a top dressing of a soilless compost approximately 1in (2.5cm) thick (this will encourage root action and basal growth for cutting material later).

(iii)   Select all the tallest cultivars first, bearing in mind that some cultivars will grow another 12in (30cm) when they are fully developed. This must be allowed for, to prevent the blooms coming into contact with the greenhouse roof.

(iv)   Secure each stem to an individual cane, making sure that the top of the cane is approximately 1in (2.5cm) below the base of the bud (the cane can be extended by using a split cane later if necessary).

(v)   If the bud is tilting to one side, cut a short length of cane about 3in (7.5cm) long and split it vertically. Use both sections to form a collar around the stem and secure so that the lower edge of the bud is being pushed upwards by the collar.

(vi)   Remove any bud bags and all ties, securing the flowering stem to the cane except the two nearest to the bloom, and then pass a loop of string or twine around the canes to bring them closer together. Leave sufficient room for the blooms to mature without touching.

(vii)   Remove all foliage up to the breaks. This will allow the air to circulate more easily around the plants and give greater access for watering.

(viii)   Start housing by selecting the plants for the end of the greenhouse first, arranging them in descending order with the shortest plants at the front.

(ix)   If possible allow a small pathway between the plants at the end and those lining the side of the greenhouse (this is useful both for checking the blooms and watering).

(x)   Never house any plants that are not good enough. It is better to give the other plants the additional room.

(xi)   Open all the vents and windows and allow the plants to become acclimatised to their new environment during the first few days after housing.

(xii)   Keep the roof vents open as long as weather conditions allow during the day and close them at night, but leave the bottom vents open unless the forecast is for damp weather conditions.

(xiii)   Aim to keep the night temperature in the greenhouse 5–10°F above the outside temperature and the same during the day if the weather is damp.

Watering must be kept to a minimum and a cup of water given every morning to each plant is sufficient to meet the plant's needs, unless the weather is very hot.

Once the plants are housed it is worth making a routine inspection of the developing buds and blooms after dark. This is the time when earwigs are most active, and the damage they can do could make a bloom or spray of blooms useless. Remove them with your fingers, or if they are in a difficult place use a pair of tweezers.

LATE-FLOWERING SPRAYS

If you want to grow this type of cultivar you should first consider what 'response group' each cultivar belongs to and the effect on its natural time of flowering.

All late-flowering sprays fall into a response group of between eight and fourteen weeks. This means that a cultivar in the eight-week group will flower eight weeks after bud initiation (early November); with a ten-week response the cultivar would flower in mid-November, and so on.

Plants should be ordered to arrive in the first week of July, and potted into a soilless compost, such as Levington or a loam-based mixture equivalent to John Innes No.3, three to an 8in or 9in (20 or 22.5cm) pot or one plant in a 5in (12.5cm) pot. They are given a stop at the end of July. Alternatively, the plants can be ordered for delivery in the first week in August and planted as before, but they are then grown straight up with no stopping.

It is important to remember that the plants should never be allowed to dry out as this encourages the stems to ripen. In the case of late sprays the aim is to keep the stems in a vegetative growth until all the buds are formed.

Three laterals are allowed to develop on the plants that were given a stop, resulting in three stems of sprays to each plant.

Late Sprays for Exhibiting

To encourage the development of pedicels bearing buds in all the leaf axil joints, giving an overall effect of a column of blooms from the top to the base of the spray, all at the same stage of development, it is necessary to restrict the number of hours of daylight the plant will receive.

Cultivars belonging to eight-, nine- or ten-week response groups for showing in early November will need to be blacked-out for a period of fourteen hours per day, starting either eight, nine or ten weeks before the required date, according to their response group. For example, if we assume the show date is 1 November and the cultivar is of the nine-week response group, blacking-out would have to start on 29 August; for a cultivar of the eight-week response group it would be 5 September. The period of blacking-out would last for three weeks.

An alternative method is to black-out for fourteen hours a day for three weeks (or until the buds show colour, whichever is sooner). Blacking-out should begin when the side shoots are between 5in and 6in long (12.5 to 15cm) on stopped cultivars, and when the plants grown straight up are 5in to 6in (12.5–15cm) tall. The disadvantage with this method is that blooms may not be ready for a particular show but it is ideal for producing early blooms.

Late-flowering sprays for cutting or decoration grown one up need not be blacked-out. They will produce a mass of blooms, mainly around the upper part of the stem, from the middle of November onwards.

Blacking-Out

The method of blacking-out is quite simple. All that is required is a framework covered with black polythene, which is placed over the plants at a certain time each evening and removed at a certain time the next morning, giving the

Blacking-out frame.

plants fourteen hours of darkness. A disused cold-frame is ideal for this purpose with a roll-down black polythene sheet. Space the pots 5in to 6in (12.5cm–15cm) apart for covering (*see* diagram above) and put down the slug bait.

Feeding

Plants in a loam-based compost will need to be fed one month after planting, and the vegetative growth must be kept going to produce the maximum leaf joints which in turn will produce pedicels for the buds. Plants in soilless compost will need to be fed earlier, starting three weeks after potting. Most exhibitors use liquid feeds of a balanced fertiliser at half strength at every feed.

When the blacking-out period is finished the plants should be moved to the greenhouse, and the stem may require additional supporting canes. This should be done before the housing, along with a final spraying of insecticide mixed with a fungicide.

Securing the Buds for Exhibition

The main stem will have a mass of side shoots throughout its entire length. You should disbud to one bud per pedicel, and the apical bud should be removed. For exhibiting you would be aiming for thirty to thirty-four blooms per spray, so count the buds from the top downwards until you have this number, and then remove all the rest.

The pedicels will tend to grow vertically as they develop, and if this is allowed to continue the flowers will be very compact around the stem. Many top exhibitors place a small roll of cotton wool between the main stem and the developing pedicel (see diagram overleaf), which forces the pedicel to develop at an angle of approximately 45°, giving the blooms more room to develop and improving the overall form of the spray.

Because of the type of cultivation required to produce exhibition late-flowering spray blooms, the normal spraying routine would have to be varied to a weekly pattern, especially during the blacking-out period. You should use a fungicide mixed with an insecticide to give protection from botrytis and pests.

Housing

Plants will need to be housed as soon as the calyx splits, so it is important that the greenhouse is prepared well in advance to receive them. The following guidelines will avoid many of the causes of loss of blooms.

Prepare the greenhouse as already described. Select the tallest plants that are not quite so advanced for housing first. Give each plant as much room as possible – at least 6in (15cm) between pots – and place them in rows with a pathway between each row, or in double rows so that the developing blooms can be inspected from either side. Limit the watering to the morning only, and just a cupful to each plant. Make a habit of looking for earwigs on the plants each night after dark.

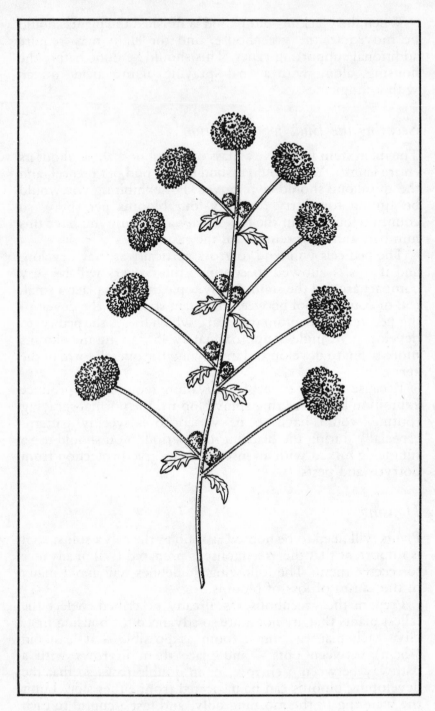

Pedicels of late-flowering spray cultivar packed out with cotton
wool.

LATE-FLOWERING CHARMS AND CASCADES

Charms

During the last few years the charm chrysanthemum has been improved in both its range of colours, and in its habit, and it is now widely used as a decorative pot plant giving many weeks of pleasure.

Plants can be grown from seed, which should be sown in either a soilless or loam-based compost in early February in shallow trays. The trays should be kept in a heated green-house, or on the window-sill in a warm room. The seedlings will start to appear in two to three weeks, depending on the temperature in which they are kept, and should be trans-planted as soon as they are large enough to handle into John Innes No.1 compost in 3in (7.5cm) pots. Plants grown from seed will be in various colours and this can be very exciting as you watch a new cultivar growing.

Plants are available from nurserymen from early February up to June and should be potted on arrival into a 3in (7.5cm) pot of John Innes No. 1 Compost. The plant will only require one stop and this should be done by removing the growing point when the plant is 6in (15cm) tall. After this, treat as for a late-flowering cultivar by potting on into a 5in (12.5cm) pot of No. 2 compost and finally into either a 7in, 8in or 9in (17.5, 20 or 22.5cm) pot with John Innes No. 3. The plant will not need to be stopped any further, and will produce laterals and secondary laterals to form a bush with masses of buds which require no disbudding. The plant will flower from late October onwards, depending on when the plant was rooted and the type of cultivar.

It is advisable to give the plant support during its develop-ment in the final pot. This is best done by inserting lengths of split canes 18in (45cm) long around the edge of the pot, and then securing each cane about half-way up with a length of green twine to form a circle around the plant. This will confine the plant to form a dome shape and the canes will become obscured as the plant develops.

Feeding should start a month after final potting with a balanced liquid feed at half strength every week.

Cascades

Due to the space necessary in the greenhouse not many amateur growers attempt to grow this type of plant, but during the last few years interest has been shown by all who have seen the magnificent displays by Slough Parks at the NCS National Shows, and at Wisley gardens. With more people having sun lounges, this type of plant would add that little extra colour to brighten up the dull days of early winter.

Plants can be obtained from seed and nurseries and the cultural routine is exactly the same as for charms, except that the cascade stem tends to be spindly and will need support from the moment it is transplanted into the 3in (7.5cm) pot. This type of cultivar must be kept in continuous growth at all times and not allowed to dry out. Potting on is exactly the same as for any late-flowering cultivar, and the difference only starts from final potting onwards.

The pot should be placed on a ledge or shelf about 5ft (1.5m) above the ground and a post or cane set in the ground

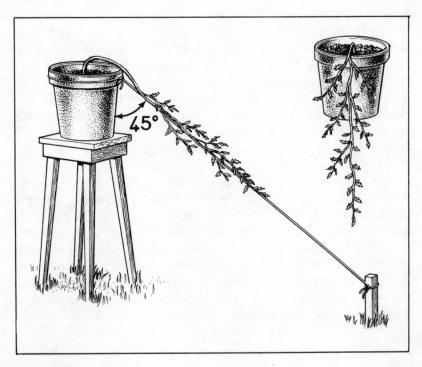

Support for a cascade cultivar.

about 6ft (1.8m) away. A cane is then secured from the rim of the pot to the stake to give an angle of 45° (*see* diagram opposite). The support that has held the stem through the various stages of development is then removed, and the stem is allowed to bend to the declining cane, to which it is secured. Laterals are stopped every three leaves, but the main growing point is allowed to grow on down the cane and should be tied every 6in (15cm) to support the mass of growth that will accumulate at the top. Stopping should cease in early September.

The main aim is to keep the plant in continual growth and this will mean feeding twice weekly with a balanced fertiliser, either in liquid, or powder form watered in.

This type of cultivar can be adapted to form any shape by using wire mesh netting secured to the pot. The growing point is removed, three breaks are allowed to develop and are trained up the framework. The laterals are then stopped, to cover the framework of the given shape.

The plants should be transferred to the greenhouse or conservatory and placed on a shelf higher than the length of the cascade; care must be taken not to damage the delicate stems when moving the plants.

5

Care and Protection of Developing Blooms

GARDEN DECORATION

Cultivars that are to be left in their flowering position for decorative purposes will require little attention. The period of flowering can be extended if stems are tied securely to supports, to prevent the blooms beating against each other in the wind.

Blooms that have died should be removed immediately to prevent the spread of fungal diseases which will be attracted. Check the blooms regularly for aphids and other pests.

Spraying over the open blooms can be done without harming the flower providing these guidelines are followed:

(i)   Use an insecticide that is not harmful to bees, such as Abal-G, if the spraying is to be done during the day. Freshly-made Nico-Soap can be used on a late warm evening when the bees are not active.

(ii)   *Never* spray flowers that need to be watered.

(iii)   *Never* spray in brilliant sunshine.

The general spraying routine of insecticide should be carried out over the foliage of the plant once every ten days, and every alternative spraying should be a mixture of both insecticide and fungicide.

CUT FLOWERS

The chrysanthemum must be one of the most popular of cut flowers because of its long-lasting qualities. However, many of the blooms will be dead at the end of a week if they are not looked after properly. The following tips will extend the life of the blooms.

The stems of the flowers are woody, so the bloom has

difficulty taking up water once it has been cut from the plant. To help the bloom and stem recover from the separation from the plant, the whole plant should be given a good watering the day before the blooms are cut, so that they are fully charged. Have a bucket of water handy when picking so that the blooms can be placed immediately in deep water and are not allowed to take up air. Before arranging, crush the first 2in (5cm) of the stem and replace the stem in the bucket for two to three hours before using the blooms.

EXHIBITION BLOOMS

Blooms that are required for exhibition will need protection from the elements. While incurves and intermediates do perfectly well out in the open, with just the bloom protected, reflexed cultivars are better grown under cover.

There are many materials that can be used to make an adequate form of covering, including perspex sheeting, dutch lights and polythene. I make a covering in the form of a tunnel, with a central ridge section 8ft (2.4m) high and the outsides 6½ft (2m) high, having ribs made from 1in (2.5cm) plastic waste water piping set into the ridge every 20in (50cm) and bent down to form a curve, then secured into the eaves on either side. Polythene is stretched over the whole structure and secured by a strip of timber at the ridge and on both sides. To prevent the ends of the polythene flapping it is secured to the end ribs by using 3in (7.5cm) adhesive tape. The polythene is 1000 gauge – a special type can be purchased which is affected less by sunlight and therefore lasts longer.

Around the sides and ends a windbreaker material is hung to give added protection, but not taken to the full height so that hot air can escape. The advantage of this type of structure is that it is not too rigid and is flexible in high winds.

Reflexed blooms grown under such covers will not need to be bagged, but some form of shading would be beneficial. Muslin suspended above the blooms and Rokolene stretched over the whole structure gives ideal protection.

Blooms grown under cover require a little more attention than those grown in paper bags because they are open to attacks from all the common pests. Careful regular inspection of the blooms themselves is vital to reduce the number that might be made worthless for exhibition. The following hints will help to reduce such attacks and avoid disappointment.

Earwigs

First signs of an attack of earwigs seem to be just as the calyx on the bud is breaking or when the first petals begin to show. The damage usually involves petals being nibbled away on one side of the bud or small round holes in the petals. The latter is not as serious, as a few petals can be removed, but when the side of the bud has been attacked that bloom is useless for show purposes.

Various methods can be used to limit the damage by these pests:

(i)   Trap the earwigs by placing inverted 3in (7.5cm) clay pots filled with straw or hay on 3ft (90cm) canes inserted between the plants at regular intervals. These pots should be inspected every day and the contents disposed of.
(ii)   These pests feed at night. If you walk around the plants after dusk, armed with a torch and a pair of tweezers, they can easily be seen and caught. Use the tweezers if the pest has retreated into a well-developed bloom.
(iii)   Place a ring of Vaseline or grease around the stem of the plant just above the leaves below the bud.
(iv)   There are some insecticides that will kill earwigs, but I would not recommend using them on open blooms.

Caterpillars

Usually the first indication of the presence of this pest is either a lower leaf looking like a piece of fine lace, or a few half-eaten petals lying below the bloom. It is important that the lower and underside of all the leaves are treated with an insecticide well before it gets to this stage. There are also several powders on the market that will deal with caterpillars, but they can make a mess of the foliage and often get on the petals of the bloom.

Green and Black Fly

These two pests must account for the majority of blooms that are discarded at show time. The spraying routine against them has to be slightly different for cultivars whose blooms are open, as they may be affected by drifting insecticide spray. I have found that systemic insecticides are ideal for controlling both these pests until they actually get into the bloom, and after that they are ineffective. So, as the bud approaches the final stage of development, just before the calyx splits, I remove any large bracts below and adjacent to the bud, then give the whole plant, including under and over the bud, a good soaking with a mixture of insecticide and fungicide. When the petals are about 1in (2.5cm) long, I use a mixture of one part Sybol 2 to 35 parts water, and spray the whole flower and the underside of the bud. Providing the spray is freshly mixed, it will not damage or mark the bloom. If the bloom has become infested during its development, it is given a spraying of Sybol 2, then a greaseproof bag is placed over it and the neck of the bag is sealed by a bag tie around the stem of the plant. This must be done while the bloom is still wet with insecticide and only in warm conditions. The greaseproof bag is removed after a few days to allow the bloom to develop naturally.

Thrips

Damage from this insect is not very noticeable on pale-coloured cultivars but is seen clearly on others as white blotches on the petals. This insect is most active during bud development and routine spraying during this period should be done with an insecticide that will combat this pest. It can be sprayed as a mist over open blooms but *not* during brilliant sunshine. Select a dull, warm, overcast day and spray every ten days.

The removal of 'cuckoo spit' from plants will also reduce the chance of an attack, as will regular spraying of any privet hedges near to the growing plot.

Bud Faults

A weekly inspection of the developing buds will enable you to spot many of the common faults which will cause blooms to be worthless, or down-pointed when exhibited. These faults can be rectified during the growing season. For example, buds that are not set at right angles to the stem should have a collar placed around the stem pushing up the lower edge of the bud. The collar can be made by cutting a stout length of cane 3in (7.5cm) long, and splitting it vertically in half. Secure a section to either side of the stem with a bag tie.

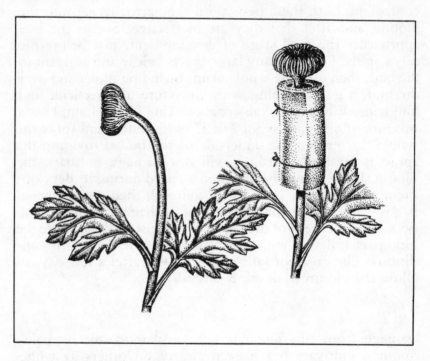

Treatment of buds not at right angles to the stem ('cocked heads').

Bagging

Exhibition blooms, such as incurves and intermediate culti-vars, that are to be grown in the open ground should be given added protection from the time the calyx splits. You can do this by inflating a small greaseproof bag, 4in square (10×10cm), commonly called a 'bud bag', placing it over the bud and securing it by means of a bag tie to the stem.

The bud should never be allowed to fill the bud bag completely before being changed to the final larger bag.

Final Bagging

The final bagging uses two bags, one placed inside the other. The outer bag is first punctured with a paper punch or something similar to give a row of holes about 3in (7.5cm) from the open end. This will act as drainage should any moisture form between the two bags. The size of the final bags can be anything from 10×12in (25×30cm) to 12×12in (30×30cm), and even up to 12×18in (30×45cm). Normally, 10×12in (25×30cm) bags are used for incurves and medium intermediates, and 12×12in (30×30cm) for the cultivars such as 'Chessington'.

Place the two bags together (the unpunctured bag inside the punctured bag), and inflate. Remove the bud bag from the developing bud and inspect for any signs of aphids before giving a good spraying of Sybol 2. Place the inflated final bag over the bud, so that when the open end of the bag is drawn together and moulded around the stem it will form a seal, and secure with a bag tie, making sure that the bud is positioned 2in (5cm) above the sealed end of the bag. Place one hand around the secured part of the bag on the stem and grip firmly, and with the other hand gently press the top of the bag down to give a ballooning effect around the bud. If the bag tends to deflate, remove the tie from around the stem and re-inflate the bag by inserting the end of a small length of tubing into the open end of the bag. This can be done to re-inflate any bag that collapses and will prevent the bloom being damaged as you try to remove a deflated bag.

The corners of the bag are then folded down to give a slope for rain to run off. The date should be written on the bags so you can see at a glance when each bloom was finally bagged.

The number of days it takes for cultivars to be fully mature from colour show will vary for each cultivar. This is the reason many exhibitors record the date when the bud first shows colour on the bud bag and then transfer this date to the final bag. It is important to record the date of colour show for each cultivar for future reference. As a general guide, early-flowering cultivars seem to fall into three categories: those which will mature from the first sign of colour in twenty-five to thirty days, those which take thirty to forty days, and those which require more than forty days.

Exhibition Reflexed Blooms not Grown under Covers

Reflexed cultivars grown out in the open will also require protection from the weather. This is done by treating the bud in exactly the same way as an incurve grown in the open, except that when the developing bud has nearly filled the bud bag, the bag is removed and a wire support frame is secured to the stem so that the developing bud is set at one-third of the height of the frame from its top. This is to allow plenty of room for the petals to reflex without coming in contact with the base of the frame. A large greaseproof bag is slipped over the frame and secured around the stem below the bud, and dated. The frames can either be home-made or purchased specially made for the job.

Incurves and intermediates that are grown under covers are treated exactly as those grown in the open ground, except that only a single unperforated bag is used which need not be of the greaseproof type. The reason bags are used on cultivars under covers is to give protection from pests and help the bloom to retain its shape.

The plants should never be allowed to dry out from the moment the tiny buds have formed, so plants grown under covers should be watered every morning to keep the ground fully charged. Those grown in the open should be watered every other day, unless there has been rain. Mulching around the plants will help to retain moisture during hot sunny days.

DAMAGE TO BLOOMS

The main causes of damage to exhibition blooms are over-feeding, sun scorching, and high humidity. Over-feeding can be identified by examining the disc of the bloom – if it shows signs of rotting, excess feeding is the cause of the problem. If only the tips of the petals are brown but very wet this is usually sun scorch, caused when the bloom has been exposed to strong sunlight with moisture still present on the petals. Blooms growing in greaseproof bags can still suffer this, when the developing bloom petals touch the side of the bag, that has become saturated by overnight rain or heavy dew, and then dry out in strong sunlight. The damage occurs to the cell structure of the petal, causing it either to decay or dry out at the tip.

Protection against sun scorching for cultivars grown under covers is given by suspending shading under the covers above the blooms, or painting the covers with white emulsion paint on the outside, and suspending a double thickness of netting on the sunny side of the covers. Blooms grown in greaseproof bags can be protected by suspending a double thickness of netting over the blooms, extending half-way up the plant on the side where the sunlight is most powerful.

Excessive changes in temperature can cause damage to blooms grown under covers when a warm day is followed by a cold night. Condensation forms on the open petals and if it is not dispersed very quickly the petals will matt together, forming ideal conditions for a fungal attack. Not all cultivars are susceptible to this form of damage, but those with a soft petal structure are. The cheapest way of com-bating condensation falling on to the blooms is to form a tent of muslin about 12in (30cm) above the blooms, extended down the sides for the same distance below the blooms. Blooms grown in bags are only affected by sun scorch when there is a heavy dew due to temperature changes.

Blooms grown under covers need as much ventilation as possible, so if the weather permits lift the windbreaker netting around the covers to allow air to travel around the plants. Also make sure that rising warm air can escape from the top of the covers or from the ends of the structure. Many top exhibitors install fans under the covers to keep the air moving but this is not essential if the warm air can escape easily.

INTERMEDIATES AND INCURVES

A week before the blooms are due to be cut for show it is important for those grown in greaseproof bags to be checked to see if the lower florets are touching the bottom of the bag. If they are, the tie should be released to allow the bags to be slipped a little lower down the stem. If the bloom completely fills the bag, release the tie and slit the bag horizontally across the top of the bloom, then slip the bag down. Tear off one corner of the bag and then tear the bag open to form a collar. Re-secure with a bag tie and then place a larger double bag over the exposed bloom and secure that. This will ensure that the developing bloom has sufficient room to allow any creases in the lower florets to develop and also to maintain the shape of the bloom. Very often good blooms are spoilt by not being allowed to develop sufficiently before staging.

REFLEXES

Over the past few years we have seen a revolution in the way reflexed cultivars are presented to the general public on the show bench, from being exhibited as grown, to well-groomed flawless beauties with every petal lying precisely in the correct position. Many top exhibitors who have contributed to the dressing of blooms in the past agree that the NCS judging rules should make it clear that when a bloom is dressed out of character it should be severely down-pointed, and only the tidying up of blooms should be permitted. However, it is worthwhile generally 'tidying up' the bloom as it develops on the plant. Some petals are unable to reflex properly due to other petals overlapping, or the petal itself being twisted. If the opening bud is checked regularly, these petals can be correctly positioned at the early stages by means of an artist's soft-haired paintbrush (taking care not to bruise the petal), and this will allow other petals to unfold naturally.

Never try to change the normal characteristics of the cultivar. If the cultivar has a natural whirl to its petal formation, don't try to manipulate the petals to lie in straight vertical lines.

Remove any damaged petals as soon as they are seen, using the fingers and making sure that the whole petal is removed. If the petal breaks off, use a pair of tweezers, gripping the broken petal as near to the base as possible and pulling gently.

Ten days before the show, make a list of all the cultivars you feel will be fully developed ready for the show, and also record all the cultivars that *may* be ready and underline them. Armed with this information you can study the show schedule.

6

Exhibiting Blooms and Judging

SHOW SCHEDULE

Firstly, it is important to understand what the show organisers are asking for in each class. The show regulations will outline the rules laid down by the organising committee and will indicate the following: latest date for which entries will be accepted; entry fee per class; staging times (the period when exhibitors are allowed in to the hall to stage their blooms); conditions of acceptance; and whether the blooms are being judged according to the National Chrysanthemum Society code of rules.

It is important that the show organisers know how many exhibitors can be expected to stage blooms in each class, especially at large shows, so it is much better for you to enter classes according to the blooms on your list which may be ready in time. This will save disappointment and possible arguments on the show day.

Many schedules for small shows are quite clear in what you may show in each class, but for the novice even these schedules can have pitfalls which lead to disappointment. For example, there are differences between shows not judged according to NCS rules, and shows that are. A show schedule for the former might call for 'one vase of three large incurved blooms'. The vase may contain three individual cultivars of either large blooms or medium blooms which have been grown large, or a combination of both. In the show judged under NCS rules the class would normally call for 'one vase of three large incurved blooms' or 'three medium incurved blooms', but you could not mix medium blooms and large blooms, unless the class called for large/ medium cultivars. NCS rules also stipulate that although a medium bloom may be grown extra large for that cultivar, it cannot be shown as a 'large'.

In a non-NCS show, the schedule will not ask for the

blooms to be named, but in a show judged under NCS rules all blooms must be named, and the judge may use his discretion whether or not to judge an unnamed exhibit. (NCS rules relating to judging will be found on pages 87–99).

Most shows have a special section for the novice exhibitor and the rules will stipulate the organising committee's requirements. Remember you can still exhibit in the main open classes in your first show. Large chrysanthemum shows usually cater for most exhibitors, whether they grow fifty or seven hundred plants, but may be restricted to members only (such as the National Chrysanthemum Society's National Shows). However, for the beginner there are many small shows that will welcome new faces.

If you have a friend who is an exhibitor, ask his advice, or join a local society. Always enter as many classes as you can. For example, a trophy class may call for 'four vases of three blooms, one cultivar in each vase', while another might ask for 'three vases of three blooms, one cultivar in each vase'. It would be better to enter both these classes, as well as four single vase classes, although you only have four good vases of blooms. On the show day you could damage a vase of flowers making it impossible to enter the four vase class, but you would still be able to enter the three vase class plus a single vase class. Also, you could find that other blooms have matured in time, and could be used in the additional classes. Normally you would not be able to enter extra classes on the show day itself, so cover yourself for all eventualities.

Check the classes you are proposing to enter and mark them in the show schedule. From the list of cultivars that you intend to show, put each cultivar alongside a class (they can be juggled around if necessary later), check you have included the correct entrance fee and post your entry in good time to arrive before the deadline. In the case of shows where entries are made on the actual day, never leave it to the last minute to make yours, but give yourself plenty of time.

EARLY-FLOWERING CULTIVARS
Selecting Stems

If spray cultivars have been grown for exhibiting, your first task is to decide which stems to cut. They should be selected to give the maximum number of blooms, all at the same stage of development and evenly displaced to give both breadth and depth to the spray. Cut the sprays, and crush 2in (5cm) of the stem. Place them in deep water for twenty-four hours before they are to be staged, removing all bruised, damaged or dying petals. Any flower heads that are 'blown' (where the centre of the bloom has matured to display a daisy eye or, in the case of single blooms, the centre disc shows signs of tiredness) should be removed, together with the pedicel; make sure that there is no obvious sign of this removal, such as a stub of stem in the leaf joint.

When selecting sets of sprays it is far better to have five or six matching blooms per flowering head than eight or more of which half the blooms are either under-developed or over the top. Flowers that are elongated or have daisy-eyed centres should be discarded. The aim should be that the staged stems of flowers will give an overall appearance of a mass of perfect blooms in equal proportions. Spray cultivars raise no problem in being transported to the show. They may be put in a plastic tub of water or, for short journeys, laid in the boot of a car.

The staging of sprays is usually done with three stems at the back and two stems at the front in a five-spray vase, or two at the back and one at the front for a three-spray vase. The sprays at the back are all cut to the same length – 26in (65cm) – and the front sprays to 23in (57.5cm) long. The back row is set in the form of a fan, with the centre stem leaning slightly backwards and the stems on either side leaning outwards. The front row is then set so that the two stems are positioned on either side of the centre stem in the back row. The stems are held in position by paper packed around them until they are securely fixed. Every effort should be made to pack each stem so that no blooms are touching and so that the overall appearance of the vase of blooms is as pleasing from the rear as from the front.

As a general guide, it is best to cut intermediate and incurved blooms forty-eight hours and reflexed twenty-four hours before staging. This is to allow sufficient time for the florets to unfold from the cramped conditions of the protective bag, and also to give you the chance to examine and prepare each bloom.

All the plants that have blooms ready for showing should be given a good watering twenty-four hours before cutting. Drums of clean water should be set out inside a garage or shed to receive the blooms as they are cut – I use 5-gallon (23-litre) plastic tubs three-quarters filled.

Cutting the Blooms

When you are ready to start cutting, a bucket of water should be taken to the plants so that each bloom stem can be immersed as soon as it has been cut. Always select at the same time the required number of blooms from plants of the same cultivar. Never mix cultivars at this stage, as this can lead to over-crowding in the confines of the garage or shed. If the bloom has been protected by a bag, first check that it has matured before cutting it – weather conditions over the previous week could have retarded or advanced the final development of the bloom. A young immature bloom will be down-pointed by the judges just as badly as a bloom that is showing signs of a blown centre. Never try to remove a bag from a bloom while it is still on the plant – wait until it is safely in the garage or shed. Start by removing all the ties, except the one just below the bloom, then hold the stem firmly in one hand and cut the last remaining tie. Select a point on the stem about 24in (60cm) below the bloom and sever the bloom from the plant. Immediately crush the first 2in (5cm) of the stem and immerse in the bucket of water. The stem needs to be crushed because its woody nature means that an airlock can form, which will result in both the leaves and the florets of the bloom going limp. Never over-crowd the blooms in the bucket – it is far better to make several trips to the drums of water in the garage than to damage blooms which have taken a whole season to grow.

Before transferring the blooms from the bucket to the drums, remove all the foliage 6in (15cm) from the crushed end of the stem. If a protective bag has been slit and a secondary bag put over the top, remove the latter first and then cut open the original bag along the top to form a collar around the bloom. Undo the bag tie around the neck of the bloom and gently ease the bloom bag down a little, just enough to allow the lower florets to settle down. Try to select blooms at the same stage of development and place them together in the same drum. Continue cutting until all the required blooms have been picked and are standing in the tubs, then leave them for twenty-four hours. List all the cultivars you have cut, then consult the show schedule and decide which cultivars will be exhibited in which class.

Selecting Sets of Blooms

Examination of all the blooms must be done with extreme care. Any protective bags should first be removed – remove the bag tie from around the stem of the bloom, then open up the bag, gently tearing from the bottom upwards. Once the bloom is free, turn it upside down and examine the lower florets for signs of damage, dampness or greenfly. Damaged or damp petals can be removed easily by gripping firmly between the forefinger and thumb, or with tweezers, and gently pulling outwards, taking care not to break the petal off. If the petal does break, the short stub can be removed by the same method – it should not be left in the bloom. The method for removing damaged petals from any part of a bloom or from different types of blooms is exactly the same. However, when removing petals from tight incurved blooms (other than from the base), the petal to be removed should be pulled gently outwards and slightly upwards at the same time.

A slight infestation of greenfly or blackfly at the base of a bloom can be removed using a damp artist's paintbrush – make sure that each insect is removed before placing the bloom back in the tub of water. In the case of a severe infestation the bloom should be removed from the rest of the blooms and disposed of.

After they have been cut for just a few hours, some cultivars can show signs of distress, due to an air lock in the stem. This should be treated by holding the bloom at an angle and inserting the crushed end of the stem into boiling water in a pan on the stove for one minute. Care should be taken not to allow the steam from the boiling water to come into contact with the petals of the bloom. Remove the bloom from the boiling water, place it immediately into deep cold water and leave it for a few hours. If the bloom has not recovered, repeat the process.

Once you have completely examined each bloom of a particular cultivar, they should be placed in matching sets of three or five, according to the number of blooms required for the vase.

The judges are going to be looking for blooms that are as near to identical as possible; blooms of a colour which is true throughout and not fading; and blooms whose shape is in accordance with the specification laid down for that section. Reflex blooms must have petals that either reflex straight back to the stem, giving a circular outline, or petals that stand out and which reflex slightly downwards. An incurve bloom should be circular in shape when viewed from any direction, with petals coming together at the top to form the perfect ball. Intermediate blooms can be of the incurving type which do not close over at the top, but show a small cluster of undeveloped florets, or of an open texture showing a small number of undeveloped florets at the crown. Blooms should be at the peak of their perfection – not too old or too young, and the size of the blooms should be within the expected size for that particular cultivar.

If a vase of five blooms is required, it is better to select the blooms for that vase first, bearing in mind that it is better to have five smaller matching blooms than four big ones and a small one. Also, try to match the blooms for colour. If you have to include a bloom which is not in keeping with the rest in that vase, never put a deeper-coloured one in with badly faded blooms, but always put a slightly paler-coloured bloom in that set.

Remember that it is easier to make a set of three than a set of five, so if after selecting the best five blooms you find they don't match, it is better at this stage to make a good vase of three blooms and use the rest to make up another vase of five blooms, with at least one spare. Once each cultivar has been examined, checked and matched, a small split cane 24in (60cm) long should be attached to the stem of each bloom with a bag tie. The cane should be positioned so that it is just below the base of the bloom and should extend down the stem to within 3in (7.5cm) of the crushed end. The blooms should then be placed in sets in the tubs, ready to be transferred into either the travelling box or tubs for transporting to the show.

Tidying Up

Reflex blooms should be examined and treated as for intermediates and incurves. If the petals of the blooms have been kept in a tidy position during the development of the flower, there should not be too much to do, but if the bloom has not been tidied up, it should be done now. (The final dressing is not done at this time, but just before staging, because petals can easily become marked.) The tidying up involves simply positioning the petals so that they hang vertically, or swirl if that is the characteristic of that cultivar. The centre of the bloom should have a small circle of undeveloped florets curving upwards to form a button. If this button of undeveloped florets is elongated, some of the tiny florets should be removed from each end, leaving a small circle.

Once the blooms have been checked, tidied up and graded for their respective vases they should be covered with a piece of material approximately 8×8in (20×20cm). Old pieces of blanket are ideal for this, as they are sufficiently heavy to keep the petals at the top of the bloom flat, and yet not too heavy to cause the heads of the blooms to bend over.

Travelling and Unpacking

Many exhibitors transport their blooms in specially-made boxes. I have found that for short distances it is better to use 5-gallon (23-litre) plastic tubs with two strips of rubber (made from a lorry tyre inner tube, if you can get it), stretched around the outside, about 9in (22.5cm) apart. Canes 24in (60cm) long are then placed inside the rubber bands, projecting about 6in (15cm) above the rim of the tub. When the blooms are in the tub, the stems (just below the flower heads) are attached to the canes, so that the blooms will not rub against each other during transit.

If you give a little thought to how you pack the blooms for transporting, you can gain valuable time to spend on the final adjustments to the blooms at the show. Always pack the blooms that require very little attention last, so they can be unloaded first and vased up immediately, in case there is insufficient room at the hall for all your tubs of flowers to be unloaded and stored while you are staging. Never try to cram an extra bloom into a tub. Make sure that the blooms are securely tied to the supporting canes around the tub and that each tub has no more than 3in (7.5cm) of water in it (there is no point in carrying an excess). Each tub should contain a complete set of blooms for a particular vase, and if the tub contains blooms from more than one vase they should be of a different colour to reduce the possibility of mixing up blooms that have already been selected.

The pieces of material that were placed over the reflex blooms should be removed and replaced with hair nets, to prevent the petals being disarranged when they are being transferred from the car into the hall.

You will need to put packing between the tubs to stop them moving and to keep the blooms from touching. Before moving off, check that there is at least 2in (5cm) between each bloom.

Staging

For staging you will need two small brushes (make-up brushes are ideal), long and short tweezers, a box of matches, secateurs, pliers, tape measure, plenty of old newspaper, your show schedule, small pieces of writing paper, a pen and a large-necked bottle to use as a dressing stand (or a specially-made stand).

On arriving at the hall, leave the blooms in the car or van and check the facilities for staging. Having satisfied yourself that there is enough room, try and choose a quiet spot away from the entrance to stage your blooms. Transfer from the car the blooms which you are going to stage first – if there is plenty of room bring *all* your blooms into the hall. If tables are provided, place the tubs of blooms you will be staging first on the table, and the rest of the tubs out of the way of people passing or other exhibitors. Collect your vases and fill them three-quarters full of water.

Your first impression of other exhibitors' blooms, either staged or in their travelling containers, will be that they are bigger and better than your own. Do not be down-hearted – you are aware of all the faults of your own blooms, but the judge may find just as many faults in the other exhibits.

Remove your blooms from the tub and place them into the vases of water. Select three blooms for the back row (in a vase of five blooms), and cut each bloom to a length of 24in (60cm). Re-crush the stems and then remove the leaves from 9in (22.5cm) of the lower part of the stem. Cut the remaining two blooms 2in (5cm) shorter, re-crush their stems and remove the lower leaves. These two blooms will be the front row, giving a fan effect when staged. Select the best bloom for the centre of the back row and place a bloom on either side, then add the other two blooms at the front. Place a piece of screwed-up newspaper in the centre of the vase, between the back row of blooms and the front row, pushed well down in the vase to prevent the ends of the stems moving. Add extra pieces of paper up to about 2in (5cm) below the rim of the vase. More screwed-up paper should be placed between the edge of the vase and the stems of the blooms so that each bloom is firmly held in the correct position.

The blooms should be leaning slightly backwards on the back row and slightly forwards on the front row, to prevent any bloom coming into contact with another and to enable all the blooms to be viewed. Once the blooms are staged to your satisfaction, cover up the paper used for packing with the leaves removed from the stems. To make sure the blooms are well staged, lift the vase up as high as you can and gently turn it around so that you have a clear view of the base of the blooms. If any of the blooms move, further packing is necessary.

Continue to stage all the cultivars that do not require further dressing. Remember if two or more vases are entered in a multi-vase class, the height of the blooms in each vase should be consistent.

Dressing

The next job is finally to dress each reflex bloom. Take the wide-necked bottle and half fill it with water. Place the bloom to be dressed in the water and pack the neck of the bottle until the bloom is held firmly. Gently remove the hair net, taking care not to displace too many florets, and with a soft artist's brush, starting at the base and working around the bloom, gently move any misplaced petal into its correct position. Continue this process until you reach the small florets around the centre of the bloom. Some of these small florets will have a tendency to stand upright, and they must be made to reflex. Gently pressing the head of an unused matchstick half-way along the reverse side of the petal should cause the petal to flick downwards into the reflex position. If the petal will not respond it should be removed completely. After dressing each bloom should be placed in a vase of water and covered with a piece of material ready for final staging. Again, remember to keep all the blooms in their respective sets.

When all the blooms have been dressed or tidied up, stage them in the vases and cover each reflex bloom again with a piece of material. When this is complete, go along to the Show Secretary to collect your exhibitor's number and class cards. Some shows issue bloom cards, but if yours does not, write the name of each cultivar on a separate piece of paper so that it can be placed at the side of the vase when it is staged.

Final Staging

In multi-vase classes it is worth remembering that an exhibit with a wide range of colours has an eye-catching effect on the judges. If your three-vase exhibit consists of two vases which contain cultivars of the same colour, never put those two cultivars together – always split them by placing a different colour between them. If an exhibitor next to you is exhibiting a cultivar in the same class as you which appears larger than yours, move your vase so that it is next to a different cultivar in his set. However, if your blooms are better, leave them side by side to attract the judges' attention to your exhibit.

LATE-FLOWERING CULTIVARS

Once the plants have been housed you will have to keep a continual watch over both the humidity and the temperature inside the greenhouse as well as looking out for aphids.

More blooms are lost at this stage of development than at any other period because of problems such as damping, petal blight, botrytis, infestation of aphids, electrical fans blowing directly at blooms and bad management. Damping of blooms is normally caused by over-feeding or extra feed being given at an incorrect stage of the plant's development. This can also attract the disease botrytis, which will attack plants that are lush from over-feeding of nitrogen. Some exhibitors do bloom feed at a very late stage of bloom development, but this practice should only be tried on a few plants until that particular cultivar's requirements are ascertained. For example, some large exhibition cultivars such as 'Gigantic' will take liquid feed at half strength when the bloom has matured to one-third out, and up to two days before being finally cut for show, while cultivars with a soft petal tissue such as 'Jessie Habgood' will not. For the method of determining whether over-feeding is causing problems, examine the centre of the bloom, and if it is black you are over-feeding.

Botrytis and petal blight are associated with high humidity, so you should keep the ventilation open in such a way that rain cannot be blown on to the blooms through open vents and damp air is not circulated around the blooms by the fans. If you set everything up correctly, the blooms will be situated in warm air which rises from a fan on the floor of the greenhouse, and is circulated by fans strategically placed above the blooms. If the greenhouse has vents at the ends and near to the top they should be opened slightly to allow fresh air to circulate.

Botrytis and petal blight are fungal diseases. In the case of botrytis, commonly called grey mould, the spores attack leaves that have been damaged and also healthy petals. Small brown spots quickly develop into large rotting areas of grey mould, with the entire length of the petals turning brown and dying. With petal blight the symptoms are similar, except that the small spots appear pinkish-brown in colour at first, quickly turning to brown-black oval areas of decay on the petals which then attract botrytis spores.

Attacks by botrytis will be reduced if the humidity in the greenhouse is controlled and a protective fungicide spraying programme maintained (*see* Chapter 10), with additional fumigation of the greenhouse every ten days using a smoke cone. Spraying with 'Zineb' when the buds first show signs of colour will reduce the risk of attack from petal blight.

Electric fans used to circulate air round the plants should never be positioned in such a way that the jet of moving air is directed at the blooms. This cold air will cause some petals on white cultivars to 'pink', and also the jet of air aimed directly at reflex cultivars will disarrange the petals which will need far more attention at a later stage. Check periodically that the developing blooms have not grown into the path of the air flow.

Even after the plants have been housed the ritual of exterminating aphids must be continued, as they thrive in the warm atmosphere. With the blooms being much harder to inspect, you simply have to assume that they are present, so routine fumigation with nicotine shreds should be carried out every ten days.

The usual practice of spraying should not be continued, because the fine droplets from the spray falling on the petals will cause damping.

An ideal method of fumigation is by means of an electrically-heated vaporising chamber. It consists of a small electrical element which heats a glass container that turns powder into an effective fumigant, for the control of either aphids or fungal diseases. The advantage is that this piece of equipment can be installed in a permanent position near the roof of the greenhouse and the glass chamber topped up as necessary.

You should always aim to keep the floor of the greenhouse dry, and any water spilt during watering should be mopped up as soon as possible and not left to vaporise as this will add to condensation. Often the corners in a greenhouse are areas where the air is stagnant, and blooms can be affected by the damp atmosphere. Try to arrange it so that the overhead fans are constantly moving the air from these areas.

Some medium single cultivars' buds, such as 'Chesswood Beauty', have a tendency to 'cock' their heads as they are developing and not sit horizontal to the main stem, so a collar should be fitted (*see* Chapter 5). In addition, the pot should be turned through 180° every two days to encourage the flowering heads not to tilt. Particular attention should be paid to any florets that are growing in the centre disc of all single cultivars, and they should be removed, as soon as they are large enough to handle, with a pair of tweezers. This will enable the hole in the disc to close over before the blooms are cut for showing, giving a nice clear centre disc.

Pots of charm chrysanthemums should also be turned every two days to encourage the blooms not to lean in one direction which would spoil the overall appearance of the display.

A daily inspection of all the blooms should be the general rule, and any petals showing signs of damping or damage should be removed at once to prevent infection by fungal diseases. Unlike early-flowering reflex blooms, the general tidying up of florets of late-flowering reflexes should be resisted – there is a strong possibility of damage to the petals which would then increase the chances of infection.

Preparing Blooms for Exhibition

The general guidelines for the cutting of the blooms are more or less the same as for early-flowering cultivars, but with the following differences.

Large Exhibition Cultivars

The cutting of these cultivars is usually done twenty-four hours before staging. Because of the size of the bloom and foliage it is necessary to remove all the foliage from the stem once the bloom has been cut for the show, otherwise the bloom will show signs of collapsing. When the foliage has been removed, the bloom should be turned upside down, to expose the base of the flower, and carefully examined for damp or damaged petals which are then removed. At this stage some exhibitors attach a support ring commonly known as a Jap ring to the stem, so that the petals are held clear of the main stem when the bloom is upright. This gives the bloom extra breadth in comparison to the depth. Remember that a length of foliage will have to be secured to the stem of the bloom when staging, so extra foliage will have to be cut to be taken to the show. When each bloom has been inspected, and you are satisfied that it is ready for staging, stand the stem in deep water until it is time to transport it to the show. It is better to stand the blooms in a place that is frost-proof and free of draughts.

The selection of blooms for showing varies slightly in this section, as each bloom will be shown individually in a vase. The aim is to match like cultivars for size in multi-vase classes: however, where this is not possible, it is better to arrange cultivars that are slightly smaller further apart, so the judges' attention is not drawn to the fault.

Medium Exhibition Cultivars

The treatment of cultivars from this section is as for large exhibition, except that the foliage is not removed and few exhibitors use support rings.

Incurve, Reflex, and Intermediate Cultivars

The preparation of these types is exactly as described for early-flowering cultivars, but late-flowering incurve cultivars are very often slow in producing the true incurve form in time for the show. There are two ways in which the development of the blooms can be advanced before cutting. One is to increase the temperature in the greenhouse by 5 to 10°F some ten to fourteen days before cutting – remember that if the greenhouse contains cultivars from other sections, those cultivars will also be advanced. The other method for blooms that are only slightly behind (where the last few petals have not quite closed over) is to water those pots in the early morning with warm water for the last few days before cutting. If the petals have not finished in a true incurve form by two days before the cutting date, cut them and stand them in deep water in a warm room. Cut a piece of light cardboard 2in (5cm) in diameter, place it over the crown of the bloom and leave until the blooms are to be packed ready for transporting.

Single Cultivars

These cultivars will require additional support to the florets once they are cut, as soon as the bloom has been examined and all damaged petals removed. The florets will have to be prevented from hanging down and becoming damaged by wind when being transferred from the greenhouse to the shed or house for sorting, and again between the car and the show hall. This is done by using a stiff piece of cardboard cut to a diameter slightly less than that of the bloom. If you make a cut from the edge to the middle, the disc can be slipped past the stem and up to the underside of the florets. It can be held in position by a peg, gripping the stem of the bloom just below the disc. The flowers should be then stood upright in deep water for twenty-four hours before being transported to the show. A second cardboard disc should be made to the same size, but this time with the centre removed, so that the disc of the flower is clearly visible when the second disc is placed on top of the bloom. This will cause the florets to lie perfectly flat. If the centre disc of the bloom is slightly oval, remove one or two petals from both sides so that it is perfectly round.

When selecting blooms for sets in this section, attention should be paid to the following:

● The bloom should be perfectly round when viewed from above, and showing a clear circular disc.
● The centre disc should show a slightly green centre, indicating that it is still young, and not dull, with yellow, pollen-bearing stamens.
● The florets should be horizontal to the main stem. (Some cultivars do have a tendency to reflex slightly towards the tip of the florets or, in the case of 'Woolman's Glory' and its sports, have a dimple at the end of the florets – this should not be dressed out.)

The number of rows of florets will vary with different cultivars, but no more than seven rows are acceptable.

Anemone Cultivars

This section is treated exactly as for singles except that the number of rows of petals may vary from one to four rows, and the centre cushion consists of small tubular florets which should be fresh to the touch. The petals may be tubular for a part of the length and finishing in a spoon shape or flat throughout. As with singles, the petals should stand out at right angles to the stem.

Late-Flowering Sprays

These cultivars will have been grown 'one up', and will have flowers projecting from every leaf joint on the main stem, giving a cone-shaped display of flowers when viewed from any direction. Normally, three stems are staged in a vase.

The spray should be cut as long as possible and then inspected for damaged florets and blooms. Those that are not fresh should be removed and a split cane secured to the entire length of the main stem (supports are not allowed on any other part of the spray). Select the stems of sprays that are as far as possible identical, with respect to the size, number and quality of blooms, bearing in mind that some of the lower blooms may have to be removed when staging. A recommended overall finished height is not greater than 36in (90cm).

When transporting these cultivars, you need to ensure that each stem is held in such a way that it does not come into contact with any other. Most exhibitors transport their sprays in a similar way to that described on page 75.

Staging

When staging large exhibition blooms the first job is to attach the secondary foliage to the stem. This should be arranged so that the added foliage leaves are just below the tips of the florets. Place the bloom with the added foliage against the vase and cut off both stems to the correct length (this should not be more than 22in (55cm)), and recrush both stems. Remove the lower leaves from the attached stem but make sure that the leaves left on the stem will hang down over the top of the vase when staged. Now fold a newspaper lengthways, first in half and then half again, and wrap this round both stems to form a collar. This will ensure that the bloom is held in the centre of the vase and, providing sufficient paper has been wrapped around the stems, no further packing will be necessary.

The general tidying up of the bloom can now be carried out, but care should be taken not to dress the bloom out of character – only the rearrangement of florets should be necessary. However, the crown may require a little more attention to produce a small knot of undeveloped florets. Some cultivars are loose in texture, such as 'Jessie Habgood' and its sports, while 'Gigantic' and its sports can vary from tight incurving to reflexing, with the end of the petals incurving upwards.

Medium exhibition cultivars are treated as large exhibition cultivars for staging, with the exception that they retain their own foliage.

Single cultivars are usually staged in sets of five and, therefore, all the blooms are cut to the same length. The stems are recrushed and the supporting discs are removed at this stage. If split canes have been used to support the blooms during transit they can be left on when staging, but make sure that they are not too thick and obtrusive. The ends of the bag ties should be neatly wrapped around the cane and stem to blend into the general surrounds.

When arranging single blooms the aim is to set them around the edge of the vase so that when it is viewed from above there is a circular outline, with each bloom clearly visible from above and below. Start by setting three blooms in position first and lightly secure them with packing, then add the other two blooms and pack them in firmly so that the blooms will not move when the vase is raised above the head. You can now add surplus leaves to the top of the vase to hide the packing.

When you are satisfied with the staging, take the vase of blooms and set it in its respective class. Replace the discs on top of the blooms which have had the centres removed, to ensure that the petals will remain flat during the period between staging and the start of judging. With a little luck they will also lie flat during the whole time the judging is in progress. Arrangements must be made to remove the discs before judging begins.

Staging Late-Flowering Sprays

Due to the cone shape of a single stem of this form of spray the aim should be that, if the class calls for three stems, they should be arranged in such a way that one stem is held vertically in the centre and the other two are placed one on either side leaning outwards, so that the least number of blooms are touching each other. It is acceptable to leave on blooms whose pedicels are attached to the main stem but are below the top of the vase, although this has been frowned upon, and may be subject to a revision of the rules at some time in the future. The overall height from the base of the vase to the topmost flower of the exhibit when staged should not be greater than 36in (90cm).

Charms and Cascades

The transporting of these types of exhibits can be a mammoth task, and you may need a van to get them to the show hall. Some form of support will have to be made to prevent the plants toppling over during the journey, and while I was in Canada I saw a very good idea for supporting charms – four pieces of timber were set on edge and nailed to form a box which embraced the pot. Because each side extended beyond the size of the enclosed pot it prevented the plant tipping over. This form of construction was also used while the plant was in the growing stage, to prevent it being blown over by the wind (*see* page 86). The cascade plant was situated in the top of a sort of high stool, allowing the laterals to fall down over a supporting screen. Two people were able to lift the whole plant and place it in the vehicle, where it was secured.

Having staged all your blooms in their respective classes, carefully check that each exhibit has its correct class card displaying your exhibitor's number, and that each vase has beside it the name of the cultivar. Check each entry with the show schedule, making sure you have not made any mistakes which would mean the judges having to mark your exhibit N.A.S. (not according to schedule). If in any doubt, ask the Show Secretary for advice. Finally, when the Show Secretary asks for the hall to be cleared, carefully remove all the pieces of material covering the reflex cultivars. There is nothing more to be done but wait for the judging, which will take any time between one and three hours, depending

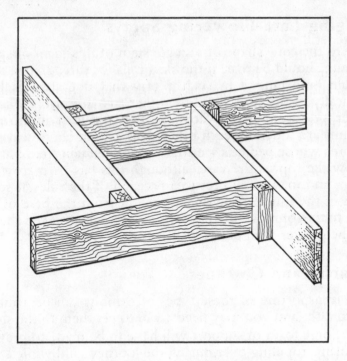

Pot support for transporting pots of charms or cascades.

on the number of exhibits and the number of judges. This period of time is useful to mark all the stems of the plants back at home that have provided the best blooms, so that next year's plants will be propagated from only the worthwhile plant material. For marking you can either use coloured wool or coloured insulation tape – I use red for plants which produced first-class blooms, blue for the next best and white for the next, and all other plants will be destroyed at the end of the season. There is no point in propagating from inferior stock, and your aim should be stock selection at all times. Having said that, many new cultivars have proved to be useless in the first year of their release and these should be given at least two further years before being discarded.

On returning to the show hall you could be pleasantly surprised at seeing your exhibit with a prize card, or you may be disappointed not to receive any award. If you have been unsuccessful, take a long hard look at your exhibit and see what was wrong. Was it the quality, size or form of the blooms, or had they faded? Do not be afraid to ask a successful exhibitor where you made your mistakes or, better still, have a word with the judge. Once you have seen your results, take a walk around the exhibits, comparing cultivar with cultivar, making notes of the winning cultivars, and making conversation with other exhibitors. Have a chat with the organisers, and find out if they hold monthly meetings and whether you could join their society. It is from local society members that you will obtain valuable information, such as stopping dates and the cultivars that are regarded as the best for their locality.

JUDGING

The following notes are a general guide, based on judging according to the National Chrysanthemum Society's judging code. Anyone seriously contemplating exhibiting should purchase *Chrysanthemum Judging and Exhibiting* which covers this subject.

Each section of classification is defined by a table, giving the judge guidelines in the form of points to which he would refer in close competition. The experienced judge seldom uses the points system in full (unless the quality of the blooms staged was exceptionally good), but remembers the points allocated to each item and mentally deducts points from exhibits as he judges. Let us consider in turn each set of tables for the various sections.

Large and Medium Exhibition Cultivars (Japs) Section 1 and 2 (Judged under Table B)

Form	25
Size	30
Freshness	30
Colour	10
Staging and foliage	5
Total	100

Form

To many exhibitors and some judges who are not familiar with the growing of Japs this can be bewildering, as no two types of cultivars (other than sports of the same family) seem to conform to a particular pattern. There are many different forms in this section, ranging from long petals reflexing for most of their length with the tips slightly incurving, and petals reflexing and twisting, to forms where the florets make a ball of tightly incurving petals, and those where the petals reflex part of the way and incurve the remainder. The experienced judge will know exactly how each cultivar should look. It would be advantageous for prospective exhibitors to visit as many shows as possible and look at the way other exhibitors have presented their blooms for future guidance.

Generally, form can be summed up as follows: reflexed blooms should have depth in proportion to width with broad shoulders, the petals hanging down either vertically or interlacing, depending on the cultivar, the overall appearance being without gaps in the florets and having a pleasing shape; incurving types should not have a skirt of loose petals at the base of the bloom, giving it an untidy appearance, but it is acceptable that some cultivars may show reflexing petals from the crown of the bloom. These petals should only be tidied up to give a neat finish to the top of the bloom.

Size

The size will differ from cultivar to cultivar but, since each bloom will be exhibited separately, any slight variation in the size of blooms of the same cultivar will not be so apparent as with other sections. Nevertheless, the cultivar should be grown to its maximum potential.

The common faults with blooms from this section is that the appearance of the bloom is either long and narrow, or broad without depth. In the first case blooms could have been improved by using a wire ring support which would have given the bloom more width and reduced the length of the petals. In the second instance, a support should not have been used, as it reduced the petal length out of proportion to the width of the bloom.

Freshness

Major faults are the centre of blooms being blown, centres that are hard (undeveloped florets), damp petals, spotting, loss of colour and tired petals that feel soft and limp to the touch.

Staging and Foliage

Blooms in Section 1 have all their foliage removed and false foliage attached to the stem of the bloom at staging. The reason for this is that insufficient moisture would be available to keep both florets and foliage fresh for the duration of the exhibition, and it also allows the exhibitor to add foliage with fewer blemishes. The added foliage should not be pushed under the lower florets but secured in such a way that it looks natural, with the petals just clear of the top leaves and the bottom leaves hanging over the top of the vase. The overall height from the staging to the top of the bloom should not exceed 24in (60cm).

The following points table covers Sections 3, 4, 5, 6, 7, 10, 11, 13, 14, 15, 16, 17, 20, 23, 24, 25, 26, 27 and 30, and Sections 8, 9, 18, 19, 28 and 29 if shown as individual blooms.

Table A

Form	25
Size	20
Freshness	20
Colour	15
Uniformity	10
Foliage	5
Staging	5
Total	100

Incurve Sections 3, 13 and 23

Form

The emphasis in this section is on form – it is probably the easiest to define but the hardest to achieve.

The true incurve should have the outline of a tennis ball when viewed from any direction. The petals should curve up from all sides of the bloom and come together to form a perfect curve at the crown, or whorl in either direction and come together at the crown, without showing a bump or hollow where the petals meet.

Size

The size should be consistent for the particular cultivar. It is better to have blooms that are slightly smaller but of the same size and form, than large blooms which lack the refinement of the true incurve.

Freshness

The petals should be fresh to the touch and show no signs of spotting, staleness at the base of the bloom or discoloration, such as pinking. However, there are certain cultivars that show a distinct variation in colour at the base even when the blooms are very fresh, and this characteristic will be taken into consideration by the judge as a feature of that particular cultivar.

Colour

All blooms should be consistent with each other, even though on the whole they are faded in comparison to other blooms of the same cultivar. It is better to exhibit blooms all of the same shade than to include a few blooms of a brighter colour in the same vase.

The overriding aim should be to achieve uniformity in blooms of the same cultivar. Select blooms that are as near to perfect as possible in form, size, colour and freshness, and never despair if the blooms are slightly down in size if they are a matching set with good form and colour.

Staging

A well-staged vase of blooms should look as good from the rear as from the front, with each bloom staged well clear of any adjacent bloom. Any paper packing around the stems of the blooms should not protrude above the rim of the pot, and it should be camouflaged with unwanted foliage or moss to give a neat, tidy appearance.

Faults

The following are considered to be faults:

- Petals at the crown that have grown on to give an oval appearance, or are under-developed forming a depression.
- The centre at the crown of the bloom either elongated or past its best and showing a daisy eye.
- The florets being uneven, giving a bumpy outline to the bloom, or hanging loosely at the base (commonly called 'skirting').
- The base of the bloom being flat, causing the bloom to resemble half a sphere.
- The bloom being tilted to one side and not sitting at a right angle to the stem (commonly called 'cocked head').

Many of these faults can be eliminated during the growing season (*see* previous chapters). Remember that blooms which are big but lack form (such as a medium cultivar grown one or two up) will lose many of their marks for form when compared with a well-grown plant of the same cultivar producing three blooms. For this reason, never under-crop an incurve cultivar, unless you have found that your method of cultivation will allow this to be done successfully.

Spotting on the lower florets in early-flowering incurve cultivars is often caused by the feeding programme in the latter stages of development. Some cultivars are more susceptible than others. It can also be caused by allowing the plant to run short of water during a hot spell and then giving a good watering, causing moisture to surge up into the bloom and rupture some of the cells within the petals. In the case of late-flowering incurves it can be as a result of a combination of watering and climatic conditions in the greenhouse itself. Most growers associate this problem with insufficient heat, and it is a well-known fact that incurves require warmer conditions than decorative cultivars.

Pinking of florets is often associated with yellow and white blooms which have been exposed to cold and blooms which are past the peak of perfection. One way of preventing this happening is to double-bag cultivars that are known to be prone to this, even if they are grown under covers. Try to plant those cultivars well clear of the outside area of the covers, thus avoiding early-morning dew. With late-flowering incurves, always try to keep the blooms well clear of the glass or corners which can become stagnated with cold air, and position the plants so they are not in the direct air flow from a fan.

Depressions in the crown of a bloom indicate that the bloom is too young – the petals have not had sufficient time to lengthen and top over to form the perfect crown. Early-flowering blooms showing a small depression should be cut well in advance of the show, and placed in deep water in a warm room with a small disc of cardboard placed over the depression. This will encourage the petals to develop.

Reflexed Sections 4, 14 and 24

The table used for allocating points is the same as for the incurve sections.

Form

Reflexed cultivars may be the type where petals reflex straight back to the stem giving the developed bloom an outline of a complete circle, while others may only partially reflex, giving the outline of an umbrella when viewed from the side. Whichever type of cultivar you have, the outline of the bloom should be circular when viewed from above. The centre at the crown of the bloom should have a small circle of young undeveloped florets, commonly called a 'button'. The size of the button will depend on the size of the cultivar, but it should never be greater than the size of a five pence piece. The outline should be perfectly round, with all the short petals surrounding the button lying flat in a reflexed position. The petals should reflex gracefully from the crown to form broad shoulders, and then continue to reflex back towards the stem to give the classical outline of a circle. The petals may reflex vertically from the crown to the tips, or whorl or overlap each other in either direction, according to the characteristics of the cultivar.

The dressing of the bloom should not change the petal lay of a cultivar, but only tidy up the florets and cover any gaps in the outline of the bloom. The tendency is to dress blooms too heavily and change the characteristic of the cultivar. This practice should be severely down-pointed by the judge.

Faults

The most common fault is over-developed blooms with little or no button at the crown. The buttons of undeveloped florets have a rough outline and may be irregular in shape. Other faults are as follows:

- Blooms not set at right angles to the stem, giving the bloom a lop-sided effect.
- Petals twisted, showing the reverse side.
- Petals showing signs of earwig damage.
- The circular outline of the bloom broken by petals protruding.
- A difference in colour from the crown downwards, especially in deep-coloured cultivars.
- Blooms showing breadth without depth.
- Petals showing signs of spotting, damping and lifting around the top of the bloom.

Intermediate Sections 5, 15 and 25

This section has four types of accepted forms:

(i) The incurving type which almost closes over at the crown.

(ii) The loosely open-textured bloom which shows the colour of both sides of the petal. A good example of this type of bloom is 'Keystone'.

(iii) Blooms in which the upper petals incurve upwards and the lower florets reflex downwards.

(iv) The true incurve type that closes over at the top as it nears maturity (under NCS rules this may be shown as an incurve. 'Gingernut', which is classified as 25b, is often shown as an incurve.)

Form

For this section form is exactly as for that of the incurve, whereby the general appearance is a circular outline. Where cultivars will not close over at the crown, the button of undeveloped florets at the crown should be circular and not smaller than a one pence piece and not larger than a five pence piece. For cultivars whose lower florets tend to reflex, they should not protrude beyond the outline of the bloom, which should be circular. Any petals that hang down below the base of the bloom should be removed.

The open-type bloom always shows a depression at the crown and will never close over at the top. The bloom is at its peak of maturity when the small button of florets is the size mentioned above.

Common Faults

Common faults include:

- Top of the bloom elongated (in some cases showing two or even three centres).
- The section of under-developed florets too large, indicating the bloom is far too young.
- Tired or damaged blooms, or blooms lacking depth.
- Spotting on lower florets, pinking on white and yellow cultivars.

Cultivars which are classified as intermediates, but which reflex due to climatic conditions or cultural routine, may be shown as reflex cultivars, in the same way as cultivars which close over at the top can be shown as incurves. Only cultivars classified in this section have this dual purpose.

Anemone Sections 6 and 26

The centre of the bloom is referred to as a 'cushion' and is made up of small tubular disc florets. The cushion should be circular in shape when seen from above, and dome-like when viewed from the side. The outline of the cushion should be smooth, with the tiny florets forming a graceful curve.

The ray florets can be either tubular, opening out to form a spoon at the tips, flat and broad for the whole length, pointed, or uneven in length. The tips of the petals may either incurve or reflex.

The number of rows of petals can vary but usually there is only one or possibly two. The bloom should be situated at right angles to the stem. The cushion of disc florets should be fresh and a bright colour.

Common Faults

- Old and stale disc florets.
- Unevenly developed cushion.
- Outline of central disc not circular.
- Ray florets unevenly placed, leaving gaps and not horizontal to the stem.

Single Sections 7, 17 and 27

(The two latter sections (17 and 27) are seldom seen on the show bench these days, however, the rule covering Section 7 is applicable should they be encountered in the future.)

The bloom should consist of approximately five rows of ray petals – some carry as many as seven, while others have only two or three. The petals should be flat, and arranged so that there is no gaps between the adjacent petals; they should stand out at right angles to the stem. Petals of different cultivars may be either flat and perfectly horizontal for their entire length, slightly curved and forming a dimple at the ends of the petal, or flat, with the ends of the petal slightly reflexing. All these variations are acceptable.

The outline of the petals should be a complete circle with no visible gaps, and with each petal lying in such a way to form a solid ring of colour around the central disc. The central disc should be free of any blemishes or remnants of broken-off disc florets. It should be perfectly circular in shape with a slightly green area in the centre.

Common Faults

- Ray florets projecting from the disc, causing the outline not to be circular.
- Gaps in the ray florets.
- Ray florets hanging down or twisted.
- Disc florets old with pollen on the tips of the stigma.
- Petals of uneven length, bloom not horizontal to stem.

Pompon Sections 8, 18 and 28

The florets of the bloom are tubular and build up into a perfect ball when fully developed. Semi-pompon blooms, when mature, are not so deep as a true pompon, and when viewed from the side resemble half a circle.

For show purposes the development of the bloom should be at such a stage that the centre still has a tiny circular button of undeveloped florets. The florets should be fresh and of a consistent colour throughout.

Pompons can either be exhibited as individual blooms, in which case they should be judged according to Table A, or in spray form judged according to Table C. If they are shown in a class calling for a stem of sprays, they are judged according to Table D.

Common Faults

● Badly-shaped blooms.
● Centres not round, or blown centres.
● Marked florets.
● Centre of blooms not developed sufficiently.

When they are shown as sprays the above also applies, but the most common fault with the spray type occurs when the blooms are massed too closely together on the stems and are not at the same stage of development.

Spray Sections 9, 19 and 29

Over the past few years the development of this section has made tremendous advances and the rules governing sprays are continually under revision.

In the past exhibitors were only concerned with the early-flowering spray which produced a mass of blooms at the end of the pedicels, forming an oval shape when viewed from the side. The development of cultivars that produce blooms all the way down the stem, and the exhibitors who have practised blacking-out on normally early-flowering culti-vars, have been responsible for the additional types of accepted forms of sprays to which judges must now comply.

There are six sub-sections to the spray section, to accom-modate the various types of bloom form:

Yellow Pennine Oriel 29a Y.

Pennine Lotus 29c Cr.

Riley's Dynasty 14a DP.

Arthur Hawkins 24a W.

Yellow Heide 29c Y.

Max Riley 23b DY.

Rebecca Walker 25a Y.

Sam Vinter 5a W.

Pennine Amber 29c LB.

Bronze Mason 7b LB.

An incurve, John Hughes 3b W.

Venice 24b P.

Debonair in a border.

Red Woolmans Glory 7a R.

Planting out.   First row planted.

Plants growing on a cordon system.

Bud bagging.

Bud just breaking.

Bud starting to reflex.

Gambit 24a P.

White Fairweather sport.

Pennine Mavis 29f LP.

Keystone 25b Pu.

Venice, Best Medium, London 1983.

Pennine Light 29d Y.

Susan Freestone 24b Y.

Pennine Whistle 29f S.

A view of chrysanthemums under cover in late August.

Redwings, an early-flowering charm.

Woolmans Star 3a LY, a late-flowering large incurve.

Shirley Primrose 1 LY.   Pennine Phillis 29b DP.

An example of the new Spartan cultivar – Spartan Bronze.

- Anemone
- Pompon
- Reflex
- Single
- Intermediate
- Spider, quill, spoon and others

There are two types of spray – 'natural' and 'exhibition'. When a number of blooms are allowed to flower on sub-pedicels from the main pedicel, this is called a 'natural', and if the spray has only one bloom on each pedicel it is an 'exhibition' spray. Exhibition sprays may be the result of growing a short season plant (late-flowering cultivars that have been subjected to blacking-out, for example), or removing second-ary buds from the main pedicel ('disbudding'), and also come from the new cultivars that produce flowers from pedicels straight down the main stem (similar to late-flower-ing spray cultivars).

Natural sprays are judged (together with classes calling for stems of sprays, either exhibition or natural) according to Table C as follows:

TABLE C

Bloom quality	form	15
	freshness	25
	colour	15
Overall effect	(includes progression development and staging)	40
Foliage		5
	Total	100

Exhibition sprays are judged according to Table D, as fol-lows:

TABLE D

Bloom quality	form	15
	freshness	20
	colour	10
	size	5
Spray quality	form	15
	uniform placement and development	15
Overall effect	(includes staging and number of blooms)	15
Foliage		5
	Total	100

Common Faults on Natural Sprays

● Blooms too compact at the top of the spray.
● Blooms overlapping and touching.
● Florets badly marked.

All the other faults as listed for an exhibition spray also apply to natural sprays.

Common Faults on Exhibition Sprays

● Small buds not removed from main pedicels or short lengths of stems left on the main pedicels.
● Blooms not at the same stage of development.
● Bloom centres blown or not round.
● Marked florets.
● Blooms touching each other or clustered too close together.
● Few blooms and no depth to the spray.

Charm Section 12a and 22

Section 22 is a new section introduced to take into account the new breeds of early-flowering charms (*see* Chapter 2).

At present only Section 12a has a table of points for the judges' guidance, but this table will no doubt be amended to take into account Section 22 in the near future.

POINTS TABLE

Bloom quality and even state of development	30
Circular outline and dome shape	30
Density of growth and even placement of blooms	30
Clean, healthy foliage	10
Total	100

Common Faults

- Plant not dome-shaped.
- Blooms not at the same stage of development.
- Blooms not covering the whole plant, showing large gaps.
- Canes protruding.

You now have a general idea of how a judge views your blooms and how he comes to a decision. Although the points allocated to the various sections will give him guidance, his knowledge of the cultivation and potential of each cultivar will be the overriding factor in that final decision. If you examine all the tables, you will note that the emphasis is not on size alone, but on form, and this should be the aim of every exhibitor. The old school of thought that 'big is beautiful' is gradually being replaced by those who appreciate blooms of refinement. Hopefully the end of the time when plants are grown one-up purely for size is in sight, (except, of course, for the large and medium Japs).

7

Increasing Stock

LIFTING STOOLS

The time at the end of the growing season is one of the most important of the year, because the decisions taken and the care of the stools will influence both your growing and success next season. Time spent in selection and preparation is seldom wasted.

Early-flowering cultivars (Disbuds and Sprays)

Once the crop of blooms has been removed from the main stem of the plant during the growing season, there will remain a short length of stem supported by the root system – a stool. It is from the base of this stem that next year's new plants will be propagated.

Some cultivars that flowered very early in the season will already be producing growing shoots. A second crop of flowers from this basal growth should be encouraged and harvested in the normal way, by cutting (not tearing off), the slender stems so that the new basal shoots are not damaged. This will give additional root areas from which new shoots can be taken later. Routine spraying with insecticide mixed with a fungicide should be continued as normal during this late stage of flowering. On heavy soils there should be no hurry to lift and store the stools – wait until late October or early November. On light soils mid-November will give ample time for the winter digging programme. This allows the stools to be exposed to a few days of frost to encourage a dormant period, essential to most cultivars, before they are brought back into vegetative growth.

The cold frame or greenhouse where the stools are to be kept during the dormant period should be cleaned out and the covers checked for leaks. The base of the frame should be sprayed with a slug killer, or slug pellets should be scattered in readiness to receive the boxed-up stools.

There are some exhibition cultivars, such as 'Chessington', 'Fred Brocklehurst', 'Bill Wade' and others, which must be kept in a vegetative state to obtain early cuttings and will need to be lifted before they are too badly affected by frost. These will require slightly different treatment.

Boxing Up

Select the stools from each cultivar that you have marked for future propagation and carefully lift each one with the aid of a fork. Shake some of the soil off and cut back any vegetative growth to just above the old soil line. Place six stools on a bed of new compost 1in (2.5cm) thick, spread over the bottom of a plastic tray or a tomato box. The new compost should be equivalent to John Innes No. 2. The space around each plant is then filled with the same compost up to the top of the old soil and the tray gently tapped on the bench to consolidate the compost. A label should be attached to the stem of each plant showing the name of the cultivar, and the tray transferred to a cold, well-ventilated greenhouse and given a light watering to settle the stools in. No heat should be applied for the first month, unless severe frosts are forecast, but regular spraying should be carried out.

(If there has been insufficient room to store manure during the earlier part of the year, now is the time to order a well-rotted load for digging in during the winter months. Arrange for delivery in late October.)

The amount of compost used for boxing up will depend on the number of stools that are being retained. If only a small number are to be boxed up, the compost may be purchased already mixed to the John Innes No. 2 formula; however, if a large quantity is required, it is better and cheaper to mix your own.

It is a matter of preference whether you use professionally sterilised loam – I have found that damp soil taken from my own garden where I have grown my plants is perfectly acceptable. The soil is passed through a ½in (1.25cm) mesh riddle and spread out to a depth of approximately 2in (5cm) on a concrete or paved area. The soil is then heated by passing a flame gun over the surface; it is then raked and treated again until all the soil is perfectly dry. This process will destroy any soil-borne pests and weed seeds.

The compost I use for boxing up all my stools that are to produce cuttings from January onwards is as follows:

4 parts dried soil
2 parts peat
1 part granite grit (or sharp sand)

To each bushel of the mix 8oz (200g) of John Innes Base Fertiliser is added and mixed in well.

After the stools are boxed up the compost should be kept in a fairly dry state to prevent the stools being damaged by frost and to discourage active growth.

For many years I used the traditional tomato trays to box up my stools, but since the introduction of light plastic mushroom containers I have reverted to these. They take up less room, fit inside each other, are easy to clean and will hold six stools comfortably. The stools are lifted with a fork and all the vegetative growth is removed with secateurs. All the soil is knocked off the roots and the roots are then trimmed. (**Note** Cultivars that have a very poor root system should not be trimmed.)

Some growers who have experienced deterioration in their stock give their stools 'hot water treatment'. This involves completely immersing the stool in hot water, thermostatically controlled at a temperature of 46°C (115°F), for five minutes and then plunging it into cold water. It is then left to dry off before being boxed up into its new compost. This method provides very effective control against white rust and kills any spores that would over-winter in the green tissue of the stool. It will also eradicate some viruses and eel worm in the stock, but the temperature of the water and the immersion time must be exact for this to be effective.

Some exhibitors, having trimmed their stools, wash them in a solution of one teaspoonful of 'Jeyes Fluid' mixed with 2 gallons (9 litres) of water. The stools are then boxed up while they are still wet. When each tray of stools has been completed, they are transferred to the cold frame or greenhouse where they are given plenty of air but protected from rain. The stools will not require watering from this point until they are moved to the heated greenhouse to be brought into production. If they do become wet they are liable to freeze, and ice crystals will damage the tender roots, but they will not be harmed by falling temperatures if the compost is kept dry.

During this dormant period it is worth checking the stools each week while they are in the cold frame or greenhouse, just to be certain that they are not being attacked by slugs or mice and that the compost has remained dry.

Early-Flowering Border Charms

The new 'Yoder' or cushion charms have been developed to withstand several degrees of frost, and so need not be lifted and stored during the winter. They should be cut down after the first frost to within 2in (5cm) of ground level and covered with 2in (5cm) of peat or straw, and next spring they will produce new growth. The plants will need to be divided up every third year if they are left in the same flowering position. However, if you want to increase your stock, they should be cut down just before the first frosts, and then lifted and potted on into a large pot using the mixture described on page 16. The advantage of this method is that it not only increases the stock but, if cuttings are taken in early November, the new plants can be flowered very much earlier in the greenhouse or conservatory, and then planted out in late June so that a longer flowering period can be enjoyed.

The alternative method is to take cuttings in early March for producing plants to flower from late August onwards.

Early-flowering charms which are susceptible to frost damage should be cut down and potted up, and stored in a cold greenhouse.

When all the stools that are to be retained have been lifted and boxed up, the whole of the area should be cleared of unwanted stools, foliage and weeds, which should either be burned or carted to a tip. If canes were used to support the plants they should be washed in a solution of 'Jeyes Fluid' and then stood up to dry before being tied into bundles for storing away. If posts have been used they should be removed and stored away. At this point I like to treat the surface of the beds with a flame gun to kill off any pests and weed seeds that may be present, so that they are not covered when my winter digging is carried out.

Late-Flowering Cultivars (Disbuds and Sprays)

Stock selection is carried out exactly as for early cultivars, discarding plants that have shown any signs of disease or weakness. Some late-flowering cultivars are reluctant to produce vegetative growth from the base, so it is as well to make allowances for this. When all the blooms have been picked, cut the main stem 18in (45cm) above the surface of the soil in the pot. This will encourage cuttings to develop on the stem, which may have to be used as a last resort.

Many chrysanthemum growers let the plant remain in the pot once the flowering season has finished and only give water occasionally to keep the plant just 'ticking over' until mid-December. However, if cuttings are required in late December (such as with some large exhibition cultivars), then vegetative growth must be kept going. I select four plants of each cultivar, which I have previously marked as suitable for propagation, knock them out of their pots and lay them on their side. Each ball of soil is cut 3in (7.5cm) from the soil surface in the pot. The plant is then stood upright and a 4in (10cm) square is cut around it, so that the stem is in the centre of the square. The four stools are then boxed up, labels are attached, and they are given a light watering. All the trays containing large exhibition cultivars, and cultivars that are slow to produce cutting material, are then placed on heating cables in late November.

The advantage of this method is that it gives more room on the staging for other boxed-up stools to be transferred from the cold frame into the greenhouse. More stools can thus be accommodated on the heating cables to encourage quick growth. It helps to retain the heat on the heated bed if the area is completely covered, thus preventing heat loss. The trays are not too heavy to lift on and off the staging, and the pots can be cleaned and stored away safely.

Late-flowering sprays can be treated and potted up in exactly the same manner.

Because late-flowering cultivars are kept in active growth by watering, the greenhouse will have to be kept in a frost-free state. This can be done either by a thermostatically controlled fan heater or by a paraffin heater being lit when the weather turns cold. The aim should be to keep the air temperature at about 5°C (41°F). At this stage a higher temperature is not necessary.

When the plants have been cut down in the pots, any surplus material such as leaves, stems and unwanted stools which have had all the old soil removed, should be disposed of and the canes treated as already described. Cleanliness is essential in the greenhouse and anything that can harbour pests or diseases should be removed at once.

If the greenhouse has not been used for late-flowering chrysanthemums before, it is worth making the effort to clean the glass so that as much light as possible is available to the plants during the winter period. It is also worth dividing the greenhouse into two sections and lining one half with a thin polythene membrane (500 gauge polythene is ideal for this). This will not only reduce the costs of heating, but will also give an area where rooted plants can be acclimatised to cooler conditions.

Taking Cuttings and Rooting
Preparation

Late November is the time when chrysanthemum growers start preparing for the jobs that will be done in the winter, sorting out all the materials that will be required for making the rooting media and the composts for first and second potting. Many gardeners collect mole hills to form the basis of their rooting and early potting composts, because this soil is in small particles and rich in fibre. It needs to be collected and stored in the greenhouse under the staging well before it is required, together with peat, grit and any other compost, so that they may warm up and be ready for use. A plant that is transferred to a compost of roughly the same temperature will not suffer a check to its growth, and the fewer checks the plant receives in its early stages of cultivation, the better the results will be later. Even the water used for the stools should be kept in the greenhouse so that it will be at the same temperature. There is little point in raising the temperature of the stools to encourage growth and then rapidly cooling them down with cold water.

Propagation

The method of propagation will have to be decided, choosing between electric heating cables or some other form of heating system. (**Note**   If electric power can be taken to the greenhouse it is an advantage, but the wiring *must* be done by a qualified electrician and the circuit fully earthed. All switches should be of the waterproof type and any sockets installed should be of the approved type for greenhouse use, preferably with a power breaker unit.)

Large, medium exhibition, and some of the early-flowering cultivars require a very long growing season and it will be necessary to give some of these cultivars a stop in March or early April. For the plant to be in the right condition to receive the stop, the root system should be very active and the whole plant bursting with energy so that new laterals are produced quickly. Plants that are rooted late and given an early stop seldom produce quality blooms. Some form of heating will be necessary to give these plants the chance to develop the strength required.

During the winter period the number of daylight hours is at a minimum, so every effort should be made to ensure that cuttings and plants receive all the available light possible. Select a suitable position in the greenhouse for the propagator, where it will not be overshadowed by hedgerows, trees or high walls and, if possible, facing south.

There are many types of electrical propagator on the market, from small ones that will take two seed trays to those that are 4ft (120cm) long. Complete electrical instructions for wiring up are supplied and some smaller models come complete with a moulded perspex cover.

The method I use to root my cuttings is known as the 'open bench method'; this means that the cuttings are never covered over at any time. I use this method because I want my cuttings to form roots and not vegetative growth, and very rarely lose cuttings due to stem rot or damping, which can be the case when using covers. The air temperature above the cuttings is maintained at 40°F (5°C) at all times by means of a thermostatically-controlled fan heater situated just above bench level.

My propagator is constructed of corrugated iron sheets supported by 2×2in (5×5cm) cross members set at 30in (75cm) centres that are carried on runners of 3×2in (7.5× 5cm) which run across the whole width of the greenhouse. A length of boarding is attached all around the outside to give a depth from the top of the boarding to the top of the sheets of 5in (12.5cm). Sharp sand is spread over the sheeting to a depth of 2in (5cm) above the corrugations, and then a 100ft (30 metre) heating cable is laid (*see* diagram opposite). The

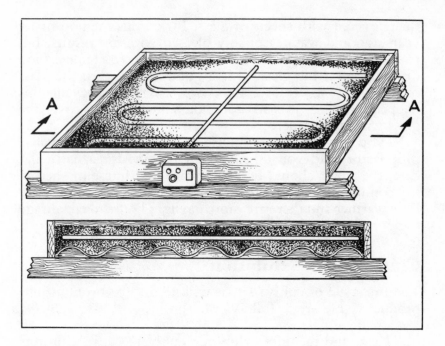

Construction of propagating bench.

cable is covered to a depth of 2in (5cm) with more sharp sand which is then gently firmed, and the bed is given a good watering using a fine rose and allowed to settle down. To the cable is attached a rod thermostat, set in the top layer of sand just below the surface and plugged into a socket. The thermostat should be set for a temperature between 55 and 60°F (13–15°C), and the whole surface is then covered by a polythene sheet to cut down the loss of heat, retain the moisture and save money.

Another method used for propagating is to set corrugated sheets supported by steel ribs above a blue flame paraffin stove, or a portable propane gas heater. Again sand is spread over the sheeting to a depth of 2–3in (5–7.5cm) and this is allowed to warm up before boxes of stools or cuttings are placed on the bed. The disadvantage of this method is that care must be taken that the lamp wick is always kept clean and not allowed to go out. Also the temperature of the bed is much more difficult to maintain.

In some cases, to keep the temperature as high as possible around cuttings while they are on the heated bed, an open-ended box can be constructed 6in (15cm) deep. This is placed on the heated sand, trays of cuttings are placed in it, and it is then covered with sheets of glass. I tried this method many years ago and was reasonably pleased with the results, but experienced the loss of some cuttings due to condensation dripping from the glass. It is a good idea to turn the glass over or dry it off at least twice a day to prevent this happening. Also, it is advisable on sunny days to cover the glass with newspaper.

If you have no greenhouse in which to construct a propagator, and you do not want blooms for a particular date, the stools should be kept in the cold frame or shed in dry conditions until late February. Then, the temperature is a little warmer and there are more daylight hours to encourage the dormant stools to produce new growth.

Cultivars for Exhibition

The first type of cultivars that will need to be brought into productive life are as follows:

(i)   Large and medium exhibition cultivars (Japs). Cuttings will need to be taken from mid–December to the end of January.

(ii)   Late-flowering intermediates, reflexes, incurves, singles, sprays, charms and cascades. Cuttings will need to be taken late December to late January.

(iii)   October-flowering cultivars that are to be grown on first crown bud for flowering late September will need to be rooted late December/early January.

(iv)   Early-flowering intermediates, incurves and reflexes. Cuttings will have to be taken from early January to mid-February.

(v)   Early-flowering sprays and charms will have to be rooted late February to late March.

(vi)   October-flowering cultivars required for late October/early November will require two stops and should be rooted late February/early March.

There are a few exceptions to the above but these will be dealt with as the procedure of taking cuttings is explained.

Cultivars not Required for Exhibition

Plants that are being grown for cutting can be taken any time from mid-February until the end of March for early-flowering disbud cultivars, and as late as early April for sprays. Late-flowering disbuds can be taken in March up to the end of April and, depending on whether one stop or two stops are given, will flower from October through to early December. For flowers for late December/January, root in April and stop in July.

Before you place any boxes of stools on the heating cables to encourage basal growth, it is a good idea to draw up two charts – one for early-flowering and one for late-flowering cultivars – listing each cultivar from which you intend to propagate. Against each cultivar is shown the required rooting date, then a blank column where the actual number of cuttings taken will be shown. On the late chart the next column will indicate the number of plants potted into 3in (7.5cm) pots, and the next the number potted in 5in (12.5cm) pots. On the early chart I use the column after the rooting column to indicate the number of plants either direct-planted or potted into 5×5in (12.5×12.5cm) plastic pots for my own use.

Having decided which of the cultivars are required first, plus those that are normally shy to produce cuttings, turn back the polythene sheet covering the heated sand in the propagator to expose only an area large enough to accommodate the required number of trays. This area is given a light watering and then the trays of cultivars are placed directly on to the heated bed of sand – the bottom heat will activate the dormant root system into life. The remaining area is still covered by the polythene sheeting until either more trays are added, or cutting material is put on to root. Keeping this unused area covered helps to maintain a more even temperature over the whole bed.

Trays or pots of cultivars that are not required until later in the month or early in the next month are placed on the staging to get the maximum amount of light. This will encourage short sturdy growth, and not the long spindly stems which are often produced when the young shoots have been grown in partially-shaded conditions. Stools of late-flowering cultivars should be given a light spraying of clean water, but stools that were boxed up in early November and have been kept pretty dry should be given sufficient water just to wet the compost but not saturate it.

Rooting Compost

The next job is to prepare the rooting compost in readiness to receive the cuttings. Mix the compost in a shallow metal tray on the staging, to keep it well clear of the floor and slightly warmer.

Chrysanthemum cuttings can be rooted successfully in many media, ranging from soilless compost, and equal parts peat and sharp sand, to peat and sawdust, and pure water. However, a compost similar to the one in which it will be potted later is the best for the plant. Since most of my composts are basically made of loam, my rooting material contains that ingredient.

(The term 'rooting' refers to the date when the cutting is actually taken and not when it is found to have roots protruding from the base of the stem.)

Rooting compost consists of mole hills, sterilised with a flame gun, and mixed with equal parts of peat and fine grit or sharp sand. When mixed the compost should have sufficient moisture just to hold together. If it is too dry, give a light watering with a fine rose and cover the compost until it is required. If the method of rooting is by directly inserting the cutting into the compost spread over the heated cables, then the compost should be applied over the plastic sheet, covering the heating cables to a depth of 1in (2.5cm).

Taking Cuttings and Rooting

For taking cuttings you will need: rooting powder, a selection of clean plastic seed trays and 3in (7.5cm) pots, a dish or jar containing a mixture of insecticide and fungicide for dipping each cutting, a small piece of wood for firming the compost in the trays, labels and marking pen or soft pencil, and the chart on which each batch of cuttings taken will be recorded. As soon as the new shoots start to show, give them a spraying of a mixture of insecticide and fungicide.

The ideal length of a cutting is 2in (5cm). Cuttings should not be taken individually, but preferably in batches of the same cultivar, to give more uniform plants to choose from at a later stage. The only exceptions to this are large and medium exhibition cuttings and late-flowering sprays; cuttings from the latter will be used as mother plants from which cuttings will be taken in late June. These cuttings can be taken as and when available.

The stools from which the cuttings are to be taken should be given a good watering 24 hours before. This will ensure that the cutting is fully charged with moisture and less likely to collapse when planted in the rooting tray. It is worth taking a good selection of 3in and 5in (7.5cm and 12.5cm) pots into the greenhouse, as well as a container in which the pots can be soaked in readiness for potting on.

Provisions will have to be made for the newly-rooted cuttings to be given maximum light once they have been potted on. Some form of shelving should be erected along the side of the greenhouse as near to the roof as possible in the cooler section. This will be the ideal position to enable the plants to become acclimatised to lower temperatures, and will not impede the light too much from the trays or pots standing on the staging.

Records for Rooting Dates

The flowering date of the chrysanthemum is governed by many factors during its growing season. The average gardener who grows a few plants for cutting and garden decoration is usually oblivious to these factors, but the keen exhibitor records each for future reference and every variant that contributes to producing blooms at their peak of perfection. The experienced grower will refer to these records to calculate the date that each cultivar should be rooted to give the best possible chance of obtaining blooms for a particular show. As an example, in two identical gardens 100 yards (90 metres) apart, with the same open aspect, where one is slightly higher than the other, there could be a difference of up to seven days between blooms maturing, even though they were rooted and stopped on the same day. For this reason each grower should keep his own records and only use other people's dates as a general guide.

Some of the factors that affect the flowering date can be eliminated either by cultivation routine or by changing the position of the flowering bed. However, although the cultural routine can advance the flowering date, the plant will always require a *minimum* number of days from cutting to maturity.

Below is an extract from the records I have kept relating to the cultivars 'Venice' and 'Mac's Delight'.

'Venice'	1983	1984	1985	1986	1987	1988
Rooted	14/2	30/1	15/1	9/1	10/1	10/1
Stopped	10/5	28/4	30/4	15/4	1/5	28/4
Secured	20/7	3/7	10/7	3/7	7/7	1/7
Colour	23/8	11/8	20/8	9/8	15/8	10/8
Mature	20/9	12/9	24/9	13/9	11/9	14/9
Height	54in	60in	60in	60in	60in	60in
Number of days from stop to maturing	133	137	147	151	133	139
Number of days from securing to maturing	62	71	76	72	66	75
Number of days from colour to maturing	28	32	35	35	27	35

'Mac's delight'	1983	1984	1985	1986	1987	1988
Rooted	27/1	20/1	25/1	23/1	22/1	21/1
Stopped	29/4	23/4	28/4	30/4	1/5	28/4
Secured	22/7	10/7	23/6	12/7	12/7	9/7
Colour	3/8	1/8	18/7	5/8	5/8	13/8
Mature	13/9	13/9	11/9	10/9	10/9	11/9
Height						
Stop to mature	138	143	136	133	132	136
Secure to mature	53	65	80	60	60	64
Colour to mature	41	43	54	36	36	35

Record sheets of cuttings taken and rooted.

I have found that to get the best possible results from both 'Mac's Delight' and 'Venice', I need to root at least 12 to 13 weeks before I stop the plants. This means that the cuttings would need to be taken between 10 and 15 January ('Venice') and 20 to 30 January for 'Mac's Delight'. The plants would be in the correct condition to receive the stop from mid to end April, and this would give me blooms for early September shows.

There are cultivars that require a shorter growing season, including 'Vision On', 'Kingstone Imperial', 'Keystone' and 'Tracy Waller'. The longer the plant has to form roots, before being given a stop, the better the quality of plant, although some will argue that the plant will become tall or pre-bud. If this is the case, record the fact and root that cultivar later next year. (All will not be lost, however, if it does become tall or pre-bud – it simply means that the stop would have to be more severe by cutting back well down the plant.) I have seen blooms from 'Alison Kirk', grown from laterals that flowered from the base of the plant, considered for the award of best blooms at an international show. I tend to root most of my disbuds from mid-January up to mid-February with the exception of 'Chessington', 'Fred Brockle-hurst', 'Bill Wade' and 'Dennis Fletcher'. These are rooted from late December up to mid-January, because they need to be rooted at least 15 weeks before being stopped to produce blooms in early September.

From my records I have compiled a list of cultivars which require a certain number of days to finally mature after being stopped and these have fallen into four categories. For example, the total number of days required by each group is as follows:

'Kingston Imperial'   110 to 120
'Venice'   130 to 140
'Murial Vipas'   140 to 150
'Chessington'   165 to 175

In the chart for 'Venice' the number of days in 1985 and 1986 for stopping to maturity differ greatly from either the preceding or following years. This was the result of freak weather conditions in June 1986 when hailstones stripped the foliage from all exposed plants. The year before, just after planting out, the ground became saturated following con-tinuous rain and very cold winds which did not encourage rapid root growth. Taking the average over the six years, whatever the general weather conditions were, the maturing dates have not varied more than a few days. Therefore, the records you have kept from last year's growing season should now be used to determine which cultivars should be rooted first. If you did not record the information, start now for next year.

Hot Bed Method

This involves direct-planting into a rooting compost spread over a polythene membrane which is covering sand above the heating cables. The compost should be 2in (5cm) thick, gently pressed down to be slightly compressed, but not over-firmed.

When choosing cutting material you should aim to select a cutting that is young and full of vitality, and not too thin or too thick. Cuttings that are old, with grey stems or grey leaves (due to dryness), rarely make good plants. The cutting should snap off the stool easily, and should be made approximately 2in (5cm) long. All the leaves below the growing point and the first two pairs of leaves should be removed. Some cultivars are very reluctant to produce basal growth and it may become necessary to take cuttings from the stem of the old stool – these cuttings should be treated exactly as if they were basal cuttings. If a cultivar is shy in producing sufficient cutting material, the best way to increase your stock is allow the cuttings to grow a little taller, then take the top 2in (5cm) as one cutting and divide the rest of the stem up into sections about 2in (5cm) long, each with a pair of leaves. It is easiest if you treat each piece as an individual cutting.

The cutting should be dipped in a mixture of insecticide and fungicide. (**Note** The solution should be according to the manufacturer's recommendation, *or* slightly weaker.) The stem of the cutting is dipped into a hormone rooting powder to a depth of ¼in (6mm), and any surplus powder shaken off, and then it is gently pushed into the rooting compost until the lower leaves are just clear of the top of the compost. The stem of the cutting is pushed into the compost, instead of being put into a hole, because you need to ensure that the stem of the cutting is in contact with the compost throughout its entire length. This reduces the chance of stem rot and gives a more balanced root system. It also explains more clearly why the compost should not be firmed down too hard when you are preparing the rooting bed.

The cuttings should be set out in rows, and planted 2in (5cm) apart in each direction (or even farther if sufficient room is available). Each row, or part of a row, should be of the same cultivar with a plastic label inserted at the start of each different cultivar, bearing its name and the date when the cuttings were taken. The cuttings should then be given a light overhead spraying to settle them in – use water that has been kept at the same temperature as the greenhouse. They should not require any further watering before the roots are formed, unless there is bright sunny weather, in which case you can give a light overhead spraying. On bright sunny days some growers place newspaper over the cuttings, but this is not always convenient to do, so I revert to spraying in the evening if the cuttings show signs of wilting – this will rarely be necessary. Cuttings will show signs of roots in 10 to 14 days with this method of rooting and will be ready for moving on in 20 days. The big disadvantages with this method of rooting are:

(i)   Some cultivars will root quicker than others and will need to be moved before cuttings on either side are ready.
(ii)   Cuttings adjacent to plants that need to be moved are disturbed and their own root development could be damaged.
(iii)   Fresh compost has to be placed back into the holes from which rooted plants have been removed, and this increases the possibility of damaging the surrounding cuttings.
(iv)   The sand below the polythene will gradually dry out and become very hot and hard, and this could damage certain types of heating cables.
(v)   There is a chance of labels being knocked out and a complete row or rows of cultivars becoming unidentifiable.

Having tried the above method, I have now reverted to using an assortment of seed trays and small plastic containers. Each container only has cuttings from one cultivar and two labels are inserted once the tray has been filled. The polythene sheet covering the heating cables is rolled back and the sand is checked for moisture, and if it is showing signs of dryness, it is given a light watering. The trays containing the cuttings are placed directly on to the sand bed, with each tray touching the next one, until all the trays cover the exposed area of the bed. If insufficient full trays are ready, the polythene sheet is rolled back to cover any area that may still be exposed.

The advantages of this method are as follows:

(i)   Each cultivar is rooted in the same tray and more likely to form roots at the same time.
(ii)   Cultivars that are not rooted are undisturbed.
(iii)   Small numbers of cultivars can be rooted as cuttings become available.
(iv)   Rooted cultivars can be taken off the hot bed and placed in cooler conditions to await potting on.
(v)   Watering can be on an individual basis.
(vi)   The sand covering the heating cables can be kept in a moist condition to give the humidity that is required at this stage.

With late-flowering cultivars it is usual only to require a few cuttings from each cultivar. I have found that a 3in (7.5cm) pot filled with rooting compost is ideal, as it will comfortably take three to four cuttings inserted around the edge of the pot. When the label showing the name of the cultivar has been inserted into the pots, they should be placed directly on to the heated sand and moist peat should be packed around each pot to prevent any heat escaping.

Many top exhibitors root each cutting individually into what is commonly called a 'jiffy pot'. These are purchased as small plugs of dry soilless compost with a hole in the centre, held together by a form of muslin. The cutting is inserted into the centre of the plug and watered, and the compost then expands around the cutting to hold it firmly. An alternative method is to use a plastic tray divided up into small individual cubes. The tray is filled with your own rooting compost, which is firmed, and then the cuttings are planted one per cube. The advantage of both these methods is that the rooted cuttings are transferred to the next potting medium without the roots being disturbed. The disadvantage is that the cuttings must be moved immediately they are rooted, because there is very little food for the plant to develop, compared to rooting in normal seed trays or on the hot bed system.

Timing

Cuttings of late-flowering spray cultivars are normally rooted in late December to early January, to form mother plants from which cuttings will be taken in late June. The method of taking the cuttings is exactly as described for other cultivars. However, these plants will not be allowed to flower, but will be cut down in May so that new basal growth will emerge to be used to take cuttings in late June. If the plants are allowed to continue growing many will reach unmanageable heights.

Cascade and late-flowering charm cuttings should be taken in late December to early January because both require a long growing season.

Other Methods

If cutting material is available, but you have no propagator in which to root plants, cuttings can be rooted in the following way. Fill a 3in (7.5cm) pot with rooting compost, insert the cuttings and place two lengths of wire into the top of the pot to form a dome. Place a plastic bag over the top of the pot and pull down around the sides until the bottom of the bag is resting on the wire supports. These supports will prevent the bag collapsing on to the cuttings. The bag should be secured around the pot with a rubber band, and the pot placed on a window sill in a warm room. Cuttings taken this way will take a little longer to root – probably 20 days, compared to those in a propagator, which will usually show signs of roots in 10 days.

Cuttings can be taken with roots already formed when they are removed from a stool. This is commonly called an 'Irishman's cutting' and is frowned upon by many chrysanthemum growers. I would not hesitate to use this sort of cutting if I was short of that particular stock. I place the plant in a rooting compost and, as soon as it has become established, I take the top section and root it again for two plants. The reason why most growers prefer not to take this sort of cutting is that if the old stool has any infection in or near the roots, this can be carried on within the roots of the cutting. By breaking off a cutting above the surface of compost, and making it grow its own root system, there is less chance of infection being transferred. My own feeling is that if infection is known to be present in that particular stock it should not be considered for propagating purposes. However, if the stock is otherwise very good with only a mild infection it should be treated in hot water before being boxed up for cutting material.

It is tempting at this stage to take as many cuttings as possible, but this will only lead to over-crowding of the plants later on, to their detriment. Take two cuttings of each cultivar for each plant you intend to grow the next season. This will allow you to select the best and most uniform plants at each stage of potting up to final potting. After taking the cuttings, dispose of the stools – and with them the temptation!

8

Potting On

The procedure for potting on young plants from the rooting trays or hot bed is exactly as described in Chapter 1 for plants received from the nursery, except that the plants will have been rooted much earlier and therefore require a little more protection and attention.

Large, medium exhibition, charms, cascades and some early-flowering cultivars which were put in the propagator during mid to late December will be ready for potting on in mid-January. If the compost is based on the John Innes formula, then it should be mixed at least three weeks before it is required. If a pre-packed soilless compost is to be used, it should be brought into the greenhouse well in advance to prevent it becoming saturated with water or possibly frozen. However, many exhibitors use a compost with *no* fertiliser added for the first potting of all late cultivars. The reason for this is that the loam, which has been sterilised, has sufficient nutrients to allow the plant to develop a good root system during the short time it will be in the small pot, without producing lush vegetative growth. Early-flowering cultivars that are to be boxed up and then directly planted in the cold frame are planted in the same compost as the lates. When these plants are transferred to the cold frame, a compost equivalent to John Innes No. 2 is used. Those plants that will be grown in plastic pots will be potted directly into John Innes Compost No. 1 (with fertiliser).

Plants grown in a soilless compost will produce roots that spread rapidly. The plant becomes robust and will need to be moved on much more quickly than similar plants grown in a loam-based compost. However, plants grown in a soilless compost will be retarded if they are subsequently transferred to a soil-based compost or into the open ground. Therefore it is better to start the young plants off in the type of compost in which they are to be grown later.

Cuttings that have formed roots will be identified by the change in colour of the leaves, from a dull bluish-green to a lighter green. At this point the tray of cuttings should be taken out of the propagator and placed in a cooler part of the greenhouse. The cuttings should be positioned so they receive as much light as possible, and kept in that position for a few days to become acclimatised before potting on.

For late flowering cultivars you can use an assortment of pots ranging from 3in to 4in (7.5–10cm). These are placed in a tub of water 24 hours before they are required for use – this pre-soaking ensures that the clay does not absorb the moisture from the compost. Early-flowering cultivars that are to be given an early stop will be grown in 5in (12.5cm) square plastic pots. The rest of the early cultivars will either be planted directly into compost in the cold frame, or in tomato trays (six plants per tray), depending on the type of root structure each cultivar is known to develop.

Some growers are now reverting to not crocking their pots at any stage, as they believe that the crock restricts the excess water from escaping. Crock is not necessary in the first potting, as the tender young roots can easily be damaged when it is being removed in readiness for the next potting.

The first potting compost is mixed at the same ratio as described for John Innes No. 1. The loam is taken from the turf stack, or mole hills, sieved through a ⅜in (9mm) riddle, and then sterilised with a flame gun.

The day before the cuttings are to be potted up they should be given a good watering, so that they are fully charged, and then left to drain. If clay pots are being used they should be taken out of water at least an hour before use so that the surplus can run off.

Late-flowering cultivars that tend to have a vigorous root system, such as large and medium exhibition cultivars, are potted into 4in (10cm) pots, while large decoratives and large singles go into 3½in (9cm) pots and the rest into 3in (7.5cm) pots. Fill the pots three-quarters full of compost and gently firm with the fingers. Lift the cutting from the rooting tray very gently with the aid of an old dinner fork, taking care not to damage the tender young roots, and ensuring that as much of the rooting compost as possible remains attached to the plant. Set the roots of the cutting down on top of the compost so that the plant is situated in the centre of the pot, then fill around the plant with compost up to ½in (12mm) from the rim of the pot, gently firming around the plant with the fingers. Insert a label in the pot, giving the name of the cultivar, the rooting date and the date it was potted up, and then place twelve pots together into a tomato tray – this ensures that there is less chance of the pots being accidently knocked over when on the greenhouse staging. Remember only to select the best plants of each cultivar and discard the rest.

Once the plants have been potted up, give a light overhead watering to settle them in and from then on withhold water until the leaves start to hang limp. This will encourage the roots to search for moisture and help to prevent vegetative growth.

The plants will not need a high temperature – just above 40°F (5°C) is ideal to keep them frost free. The roof vents should be opened slightly when the weather permits, but avoid standing the plants in a draught.

Early-flowering cultivars that require an early stop are better grown in 5in (12.5cm) plastic pots in the greenhouse where it is slightly warmer. After they are stopped, the laterals get away much more quickly. After about a month, and after stopping, these plants will need supplementary feeding to encourage new growth. Once the plants show signs of growth they should be given as much room as possible between them. The routine spraying of insecticide and fungicide should be continued even though there appears to be no visible signs of an attack. The confines of the greenhouse make the inspection of individual plants more difficult as they develop, but a constant watch must be maintained for slugs at all times.

ASH BASE METHOD

The ash base method of cultivation, prior to planting out, has become very popular with most of the leading national exhibitors. Each grower may have his own slight variation on the amount of fertiliser used, or how thick the compost should be, but the principles are similar.

Having tried various combinations of thickness of compost and varying strengths, I have come to the conclusion that my cuttings grown in 5in (12.5cm) pots produced plants which were much on par with those grown on the ash base method. Because of the space needed, I grow cultivars that need a shorter growing season on the ash base method, and those that call for a long season in plastic pots.

The cold frame used for the ash base method need not be of a brick construction, but it must be frost proof and in a position to obtain the maximum light. The inside of the frame should be painted, either with a lime wash or a white emulsion paint. A bed of washed ashes 3–4in (7.5–10cm) thick is spread over the whole area of the frame base and compacted. An alternative material for the base is pea gravel spread to a depth of 2in (5cm) and covered with either 1in (2.5cm) of sharp sand or a perforated plastic sheet. This will prevent the gravel becoming mixed with the compost.

The compost should be mixed three weeks before it is required to a formula equivalent to John Innes No. 2. It should be spread over the top of the ash base to a depth of 4in (10cm) and lightly firmed. I place a piece of timber 4in (10cm) thick along each side of the bed, and with another piece of timber I scrape the compost between these two timbers to a constant thickness and also to keep the surface of the bed as level as possible. The two lengths of timber from the edges of the bed are then removed, and the gaps left are filled level with the rest of the bed. Once the bed has been prepared, the covers should be cleaned (if they are glass), and replaced to allow the compost to warm up in readiness to receive the plants.

Transferring the plants to the ash base is done in the first few days in March, but this should not coincide with severe weather conditions. It would be better to delay planting out by a few days than risk the plants being damaged by a hard frost. If possible, planting out should be done without standing on the compost within the frame. However, if this is unavoidable, use a short plank to spread the weight and so avoid compressing the compost.

The plants will look rather small when they are ready to be planted out, but remember that they will be growing in this frame for seven to eight weeks, so they should be given as much room as possible. I use a marked length of wood 8in (20cm) wide and slightly shorter than the width of the frame, to help me position the plants within the frame. The first row of plants is placed 4in (10cm) in from the sides and ends of the frame. The piece of timber is placed alongside the first row and the next row of plants is positioned 8in (20cm) from the first row. Plant in short rows across the frame, inserting a label at the beginning and end of each batch of cultivars, and draw up a chart indicating which row contains which cultivar. This will save time and possible damage when searching for the cultivars that need to be stopped whilst they are still in the frame.

Give the plants a liberal watering, preferably in the morning and scatter a few slug pellets between the plants. The covers should be placed back on the frames and secured.

PROTECTION

Frosts are bound to occur during March, so contingency plans will have to be made to prevent the plants from becoming damaged. This will mean covering over the frames whenever necessary with some suitable material. Old carpets or sacks are ideal, but they do become rather heavy and extremely difficult to dry out once they are wet. If they are cut to fit inside polythene bags which are sealed with a length of adhesive tape, they are just as effective but stay dry. Be sure they are securely held down, otherwise the wind will easily blow them off, leaving the glass or polythene covers unprotected.

The plants will not require watering for at least 3 to 4 weeks, and any signs of leaves hanging limp during a warm spell should be ignored, as long as the plants are checked the next morning to see that they have perked up. If not, this is the time to give them the next drink, otherwise leave them alone except for the regular spraying.

The covers should be left on for the first 10 to 15 days, and after this period only opened a few inches if the weather conditions permit.

If there is snowfall during March or early April, the snow should not be removed from the covers unless this is likely to make the covers collapse. The plants will come to no harm, and the snow will act as insulation against extreme changes in temperature, giving your plants further protection.

ADVANTAGES OF DIRECT-PLANTING

(i) Roots are allowed to run freely and will develop into enormous root systems.
(ii) Plants require minimal attention whilst they are in the cold frame.

DISADVANTAGES OF DIRECT-PLANTING

(i)   Fewer plants are accommodated in the frame.
(ii)   Damage to roots is possible whilst they are being lifted for replanting.
(iii)   A large amount of compost needs to be mixed to give the necessary thickness of base.
(iv)   There may be problems with some cultivars reaching the underside of the covers, if the depth of the frame is too shallow.
(v)   It is more difficult to examine a particular plant.

So, if you have the room, use the ash base method for cultivars that do not require a long growing season and are intended for exhibition.

NEXT POTTING STAGE

Late-flowering cultivars which were potted up in early January will require moving into the next pot from mid-February onwards. As with the first potting, different sizes of pots will be required. The compost to be used should be equivalent to John Innes No. 2 (*see* Chapter 1). Large exhibition cultivars are potted into 6in (15cm) pots, and all the remaining plants into 5in (12.5cm) pots. The potting procedure is exactly as for the first potting. If some plants are now becoming tall they should have a short split cane inserted into the compost approximately 1in (2.5cm) from the stem, and the plant should then be secured to the cane by tying a loop of string or raffia around the cane and stem of the plant.

GROWTH-RETARDING AGENTS

(Many exhibitors and nurserymen use retarding agents to restrict the height of plants in the early stages of growth. Some of these agents have been available to the amateur, but in the near future they may not be available under the names given here due to the fact that a new Pesticides Act is coming into force.)

Gro-Slo is one retarding agent which is useful. It is mixed in a ratio of 20 parts water to 1 part Gro-Slo, and sprayed as a very fine mist on to the leaves and stems of plants when they are potted into their first pots. They are given a second spray at the 5–6in (12.5–15cm) pot stage. Care should be taken to avoid excess liquid running on to the surface of the compost – lay the plants on their sides to allow any surplus to drain off.

Plants that require watering should not be treated but given a good watering and then treated the next day. The plant's foliage should be kept dry for 24 hours after treatment and therefore it should be kept well clear of any overhead watering which may be given to other plants. Spraying of retarding agents should never be carried out in brilliant sunshine; try to choose a dull, overcast day. Never spray outside in windy conditions, but choose a still day to avoid drifting spray settling on other plants. Plants that are due to be stopped should not be treated within a month of the required stopping date.

The aim of this treatment is to produce short sturdy plants with leaf joints very close together. If it is applied to laterals when they are 18in (45cm) long, it will reduce the overall height of the plant by as much as 24in (60cm). This makes some tall cultivars more manageable at housing time.

Retarding agents are also particularly useful for strengthening the necks of cultivars which are renowned for being too weak to support large blooms. The solution is made at the ratio of 10 parts water to 1 of Gro-Slo. When the bud is secured, the solution is applied to the stem, below the bud down to the first pair of leaves, with an artist's paintbrush. This causes the stem to thicken and reduces its length.

SAFETY AND HYGIENE

When using any insecticide or chemicals of this nature, be sure to wear rubber gloves, goggles and a face mask. Store the chemical in a safe, locked cupboard, well out of the reach of children. Give the sprayer a good wash out before it is put away, even if you do keep it solely for that purpose. This general hygiene will prevent residues building up which could be harmful to the plants the next time the sprayer is used.

9

Growing Media

LOAM

Basically, loam is the portion of soil which incorporates fibrous grass roots. The particles or grains of soil are the remnants of eroded sedimentary or volcanic rocks mixed with rotted vegetation. The individual particles may be of sand derived from sandstone or clay deposited by water action. Sometimes the make-up can be a mixture of both. It is usually believed that if the particles are slightly greasy and smooth to the touch, rather of the same nature as clay, the loam is desirable for compost. The particles should be not too small and yet not too fine; they should bind together and form an impervious mass.

The ever-increasing cost of good quality loam has resulted in many chrysanthemum growers experimenting with other materials to replace the traditional loam-based composts. The results have varied, from very poor in the beginning to extremely good once growing techniques have been adapted to the new composts.

All that chrysanthemums need to grow and produce blooms is a medium in which the roots can forage for moisture and nutrients, and which can act as an anchorage for the plant. The quality of the flowers produced will depend on the availability and quantity of the nutrients within that medium. Some loam substitutes, such as sawdust, have been tried with all the correct ingredients incorporated. The results in the beginning were very poor, because the amount of nitrogen in the compost was insufficient to support the plant. However, as the amount of nitrogen was increased both the vigour of the plant and quality of the blooms improved. It was also found that different types of sawdust required different amounts of nitrogen to achieve the same results.

Peat/sawdust combinations have also been the subject of experimentation, and the results are very promising. As with pure sawdust composts, calculating the correct ingredients to be added proved difficult, and this resulted in plants that were either too lush, or very weak and requiring liquid feeding early on.

PEAT-BASED COMPOSTS

The first major problem encountered with peat-based compost that had not been treated to absorb water was that it dried out too quickly. Most growers are not at home during the day, and many returned to find their blooms in the greenhouse ruined after a warm day. The manufacturers have now overcome this problem by adding a wetting agent to the compost. Anyone contemplating mixing their own peat-based compost from pure peat should also add some form of wetting agent to the mix (for mixing instructions, see Chapter 1).

Peat-based composts tend to run out of feed very much more quickly than loam-based composts, so feeding has to be introduced very much earlier. Plants in loam-based compost in their final pots would normally be fed four weeks after potting, but with soilless compost this needs to be done at least 10 days sooner in order to maintain the plant's momentum.

Root action is much quicker, and races through the compost using up the fertiliser very rapidly. This results in the foliage becoming very lush, and if this is allowed to continue it will lead to disastrous results. The process of gradual ripening of the plant has to be carried out with the aid of potash liquid feeds if the plant shows signs of becoming out of balance. With loam-based composts, it is very much easier to keep the plant in balance and ripen the plant by restricting the amount of water given. This is achieved by allowing the compost to partially dry out, but this method could cause problems with peat-based composts which are reluctant to absorb water after drying out.

Watering is the major problem with soilless composts – knowing when to do it or when to withhold. The old method of tapping the clay pot is useless. The decision has to be made based on observation, and this can be misleading – the surface of the compost can look quite dry, yet below the surface it could be really wet. Soilless compost also tends to dry out much more quickly in clay pots than in plastic ones.

Canes inserted in soilless compost at the final potting stage can be a problem if they are not secured to the straining lines immediately. Because of the looseness of the material they tend to flop around and do not give sufficient support to the plant in the early stages. They will become more stable as the compost compacts with watering, and the roots will help to bind the compost together as they progress through it. One of the great advantages of using a soilless compost is its weight in relation to a loam-based compost. Not having to carry heavy pots at housing time is a big advantage, especially if you have a large number to handle.

WOOD BARK / PEAT
MIXED COMPOSTS

There is a product on the market called 'Cambark' which is a 50/50 mix of peat and bark, for multi-purpose use. The mixture consists of particles of bark from softwood trees (ranging from 1/8in (4mm) to dust), mixed with sphagnum peat. The manufacturers say that, in addition to the fertiliser used for general plant growth, an amount of nitrogen in the form of ammonia nitrate must be added, at the rate of 0.035oz (1g) per 1.77 pints (1 litre) of mix used. In other words, for every bushel of mixture used you would need to add 6.3oz of ammonia nitrate, plus the normal amount of fertiliser for that specific mix.

This is again a soilless compost, and it has given some excellent results from experiments carried out by some of the leading top growers. It could well replace the traditional loam-based compost as a growing medium for chrysanthemums in the future. Growers have had to learn new techniques with this combined compost, as well as overcoming the problems of growing in a soilless compost.

This new medium has a more open-type structure, and yet has the capacity to retain sufficient moisture without completely excluding the air. In this way the roots are allowed to take in nutrients more readily and to breathe more freely. Unlike a pure peat compost 'Cambark' retains its open structure throughout its entire use, and yet is relatively slow in drying out. It is obviously worth trying out a few plants in it.

HOW TO MAKE
YOUR OWN LOAM

Many of us cannot obtain loam of the right quality in the right quantity at the time it is required. So, to be sure that you have sufficient loam, it is better to produce your own. I prepare to build my stack in July for the next year's final potting, but on occasions I have left it until October, when I use well-rotted manure as alternative layers.

Type of Material

The ideal turf would be that cut from a well-drained meadow that has been grazed for a number of years, where the soil is of a slightly clay nature. With the increase in meadow lands being ploughed for cereal crops, the chance of finding the ideal turf is very remote. I either contact a local landscape gardener and ask if he can supply a load of turf offcuts, or if I see a field being stripped by a turf contractor I ask if I can purchase any odd pieces of turf that are not required. There are usually plenty lying around which they are happy to get rid of. Alternatively I order squares of turf. If you do this, be sure to ask if a selective weedkiller has been used – I have seen plants killed by composts made from turf that has been treated with weedkiller.

Construction of the Loam Stack

The material for the loam stack should be tested for its pH before being used. The loam stack should be as near to the recommended reading of 6.5 as possible when ready for use. If the turf or soil to be used shows a pH reading of lower than 6, this means that the material is slightly acid, and it will become more acid as the manure is added. Hydrated lime should be added at the rate of 3oz (85g) sprinkled over every square yard (square metre) of the surface area of the stack, for every 12in (30cm) in height. This will raise the pH by approximately 0.5. If the material shows a reading in excess of 7, then a 1in (2.5cm) layer of peat should be spread over the surface area of the stack for every 12in (30cm) in height.

Choose a spot approximately 48×36in (120×90cm) to stack the turf. It should be well drained, and if possible you should put a layer of either ash or gravel over the area to give extra drainage. Place a layer of turf or off-cuts 6in (15cm) thick over the prepared area, laying them upside-down so that the grass roots are exposed. Put a layer of manure on top (fresh will be ideal), and every fourth layer of turf give a light dusting of lime, just to keep the compost sweet. Continue building up the stack with alternate layers until all the turf has been used. Soil that was delivered with the turf can be put in the stack.

The sides of the stack should lean slightly towards the centre of the pile to encourage rain to run off. When the stack is completed, a cover should be placed over the top (a corrugated sheet is ideal) to prevent the rain penetrating the heap, but the sides should not be covered. This will allow air to penetrate the stack freely and speed up the process of breaking the turf down into a rich loam.

For many years gardeners have used the soil from their plots to grow seedlings for planting out in the spring. Providing the plot is well maintained and managed carefully, there is no reason why soil from the plot should not be used to make loam, unless it consists of fine particles of light sandy soil. If this is the case, mix the sandy soil with some very clay-like soil. On the other hand, if the garden plot is of the very sticky clay type, it should be mixed with sharp sand in equal proportions as the stack is being built.

In your loam you should be looking for plenty of fibre. Normal garden soil will be short of this, so it needs to be added by using leaves, straw or manure, or a combination of any of these. Grass cuttings can be used, but I prefer to put my grass cuttings in a pile to decompose and then incorporate them with manure into the plot.

Leaves collected in the autumn should be placed in plastic bags and stored under a hedgerow with the bags left open. In early spring start building the loam stack by laying a carpet of manure 6–12in (15–30cm) thick over the area which has been set aside for the purpose, then spread a layer of soil 4in (10cm) thick on top followed by 2oz to the square yard (56 grams per square metre) of coarse bonemeal. Water the area using a fine rose on the watering can and cover with a layer of leaves from the stored sacks. Continue building the heap up to a height of 48in (120cm), with alternate layers, adding the coarse bonemeal after each layer of soil and watering in. Cover the stack with polythene sheeting held down by bricks and leave for twelve months. It will be ideal for final potting next year.

It is important to test the pH of the loam stack well in advance of it being required, so that any adjustments can be made before the loam is used to make compost. Aim for a reading of 6.5 at the beginning, rather than find out later that the pH is way out and the plants are suffering. Having said that, I have seen chrysanthemums growing quite happily in a very alkaline soil with a reading in excess of 7.5, but this requires a great deal of experience and clever feeding.

10
Pests, Predators, Diseases and Deficiencies

PESTS

Ants

Not usually regarded as a problem on chrysanthemums that are kept free of greenfly, but ants are known to transport greenfly from plant to plant and to milk them to extract the sugary substance they secrete.

The nest can be dealt with in two ways: by puffing 'Nippon' in and around the entrance if the nest is near to the plants, or, if the nest is at a distance from the plant's roots, by pouring boiling water into the nest entrance.

Aphids

Whenever chrysanthemum growers get together, sooner or later the conversation will turn to this common persistent pest, which is responsible for many good exhibits being discarded.

There is no dormant period for the aphid, so throughout the whole year vigilance cannot be relaxed against an attack. Even in the depths of winter, when the temperature in the greenhouse is very low, these pests can become established.

Black Bean Aphid

These black aphids are commonly seen on the main stem of an individual plant in large colonies, but rarely spread to other plants. Eradication of this type is easily carried out by spraying with either 'Sybol 2', 'Tumblebug' or 'Rapid'.

Chrysanthemum Aphid

Light brown in colour, these usually attack the stems first, and then the leaves, before moving up the stem to the bud. Although a little harder to eradicate than the black bean aphid, spraying every ten days with either of the above-mentioned insecticides will kill any infestation quickly.

Leaf-Curling Plum Aphid

These are small green aphids usually found in the growing point of the chrysanthemum and under the bracts of the buds. They usually set up colonies within the lower florets of developing blooms, and particular attention should be given to spraying this part of the plant at all times, especially prior to bagging.

Mottled Arum Aphid

This is commonly found on other flowers and only occasionally on chrysanthemums. This aphid is a shiny green and usually found on tender young leaves and shoots. Spraying with insecticides, as mentioned above, will clear up any infestation.

Peach Potato Aphid

This is the most commonly-known type of all the species and attacks a wide range of plants in the garden, house and greenhouse. The colour may vary from green to light yellowish-green. They start their attack usually on lower leaves and tender young shoots, and gradually advance up the plant. An infestation of ants on a plant is a good indication that these aphids are present. It is known that this type of aphid can become immune to insecticides, so it is recommended to alternate the insecticide used at each routine spraying. It is better to prevent aphids attacking plants than having to deal with an infestation. Aphids feed by puncturing the tissue of the plant and sucking the sap, and this is responsible for the spread of some virus infections found in plants.

In addition to the normal method of spraying, there are systemic insecticides that can be applied either by watering the diluted mixture on to the ground, or by direct spraying on to the plant. Insecticides such as Boots 'Greenfly and Blackfly Killer' and Murphy's 'Tumblebug' are ideal for spraying on to the plants. The disadvantage of spraying is that some pests escape the spray to continue their breeding cycle, whilst aphid predators are also killed. Also, most of the contact insecticides have a very limited life, especially in a wet season. The poison in systemic insecticides, on the other hand, is circulated within the sap stream of the plant, and is therefore only available to pests that feed by sucking and not harmful to aphid predators. The only disadvantage is that pests can still spread virus infections before they are killed.

There is increasing pressure on gardeners to restrict the amount of spraying carried out because of the harmful effects it has on insects that are helpful to the gardener. Therefore, every effort should be made to limit the use of insecticides that kill both pests and predators. The general spraying routine should be carried out by using insecticides that are not harmful to predators but act as a deterrent, and systemic insecticides should be used as a back-up. Systemic insecticides will not protect blooms, and these will need to be sprayed with insecticides (*see* page 63).

Birds

Since I have three cats, it is not surprising that I have never experienced the problem of birds removing growing tips from young plants, but I know this can be a problem to some growers. The simplest way to combat this problem is to stretch lengths of string above the plants and short strips of plastic to them. These will flap in the breeze and deter the birds. Fine netting stretched over supporting canes above the plants is also a good deterrent.

Caterpillars

The colour of caterpillars may vary from lightish brown to bright green, depending on the moth species. The eggs of the moths are laid on the underside of lower leaves and usually go unnoticed, until the surface area of the leaf becomes transparent because of the tiny caterpillars eating the tissue of the leaves. When the leaf is turned over it will be smothered with thread-like worms. Larger caterpillars chew leaves and large areas of petals, and the first indication of their presence is half-eaten petals and droppings on the leaves. It is difficult to detect this pest because its colouring acts as a camouflage amongst the foliage, but on closer inspection it can be found either in the bloom or on the foliage. Late evening is the best time to catch this pest feeding.

Normal insecticides are not very effective against the larger caterpillars unless they actually eat the sprayed areas. For this reason it is essential that both the top and undersides of the leaves are completely sprayed with an insecticide containing *Bacillus thuringiensis*, such as 'Atlas Herbon Thuricide'. Small caterpillars can be killed with 'Liquid Derris' or any similar brands.

Cutworms

The first indication of an attack by these pests is that the leaves hang limp, giving the impression that the plant needs water. On investigation, however, the stem of the plant just above the surface of the soil will show signs of being partially severed. If 'Bromophos' is sprinkled over the soil surface, and then gently hoed in during August, it will prevent the moth laying its eggs in the soil.

Chafer Beetles

The signs of an attack are similar to those indicating cutworms, but the stem may show signs of the attack just *below* the surface of the soil or the roots may have been eaten. If the soil surrounding the plant is dug up, the culprit, a large whitish grub with a dark brown head and six legs, is usually found. The larvae are often transported to the garden in topsoil or leaf mould. If the plants show only a slight attack the soil should be given a good watering of BHC solution.

Earwigs

These pests attack the developing buds and buds that are showing colour by nibbling the ends of the florets and petals of open blooms. They are very active at night and can be seen, with the aid of a torch, feeding on the blooms. They are found anywhere in the garden where there is a suitable hiding place – in piles of leaves under the hedge, amongst old timber and bricks.

The best way to eliminate these pests is by catching them at night. Another method is to place small inverted pots filled with hay, or rolls of corrugated paper fixed with an elastic band, on canes between the plants. Each morning the traps should be examined and the occupants dealt with.

Eelworms

These pests are not visible to the naked eye and the attack is only noticed when triangular black areas appear on the lower leaves which gradually progress up the plant. These triangular areas are caused by tiny worms feeding between the tissue and veins of the leaves. They can infect the whole plant within a few days during a wet season. Plants showing signs of eelworm attack should be dug up, together with the surrounding soil, and burnt. Chrysanthemum stools should be given hot water treatment to prevent the pests over-wintering in the stool tissue (*see* page 102). Any area showing signs of eelworms should be either sterilised or left free of chrysanthemums for at least three years.

Froghoppers

Inside the balls of foam commonly known as 'cuckoo spit' are small bright green insects. The insect forms this foam by sucking sap from the plant, and in early summer it develops into a brown adult insect that jumps from plant to plant. The effect of this insect's feeding habits leaves white areas on the leaves, and buds being deformed. The best control is by regular spraying with a contact or systemic insecticide.

Leaf Miner

The first indication of the presence of leaf miner is small white dots appearing on the surface of the leaves. These dots are puncture marks where the adult flies have been feeding, and where the female will deposit an egg that will later turn into a small lava, which will burrow in the tissue between the upper and lower leaf surface leaving a white twisting trail. This disfigurement of the leaf can be slight or very severe, and in some cases the whole plant is affected, rendering the bloom virtually useless for show purposes.

If the plants are sprayed regularly with an insecticide containing Dimethoate, on an alternating basis with other insecticides, they should remain free of this pest. If the attack is only slight, I have found it best to turn the leaf over and simply remove the small larva before it has had time to disfigure the leaf too badly.

Mirids (Capsids)

The common green capsid is usually very active during the warm summer months. It attacks by biting into the stems and leaves, causing distortion to the leaves and stunting the growth of the growing tip. When buds are attacked the flower is often deformed. This pest over-winters as an egg laid in weeds, so it is important to keep the area free from weeds at all times. Spraying over and under the leaves with an insecticide containing Fenitrothion will keep this pest at bay.

Mice

Not usually a problem during the summer months, but mice can become a menace during the winter in a cold frame or greenhouse if the weather turns very cold for long spells. They will eat tender young shoots from stools and young cuttings, so examination of boxed-up stools should be made periodically for signs of damage. If an attack is evident then appropriate bait should be set.

Moles

These creatures are not a problem in built-up areas where the garden has been cultivated regularly, unless the garden is adjacent to grazing land where moles are active. They soon become interested in the garden if it has been well manured, looking for worms. The damage they cause is by tunnelling under the plants often causing the plants to wilt and die. The only effective method is to trap them.

Red Spider Mite

These are more commonly associated with greenhouse chrysanthemums than outdoor plants, but occasionally in very warm weather an attack can occur. The leaves take on a mottled appearance where the insect has punctured the leaves, and the growing point will be covered with a fine web. Spray with any of the leading insecticides.

Stool Miner

Attacks from this pest are not so common, due, I believe, to continual hoeing between the plants in the early stages of growth. This discourages the small black fly from laying its eggs in the soil near to the plants during May and June.

If eggs are laid, when they hatch out the small grubs feed on the roots, and make tunnels in the stem of the plant just below the bark. There they turn into pupae, and remain for a while, before reappearing in August to start the laying sequence all over again. The second brood of eggs will hatch out in time for the grubs to be well concealed within the stem of the plant where they will feed throughout the winter period. If the stools are hot water treated before being boxed up in the autumn these pests will be killed off. A top dressing of 'Bromophos' worked into the top 2in (5cm) of soil in mid–May, followed by another dressing in August will deter the flies from laying eggs.

Slugs and Snails

Fortunately, attacks by these pests can be fought very quickly if precautions are taken. The relatively new liquid form of slug killer is ideal for killing off the slug eggs, if it is applied to the areas in late autumn where slugs are known to hide. Favourite slug breeding places are under bricks, old timber and garden rubbish. The eggs can either be collected and disposed of, or burnt with a flame gun. Each find will reduce next season's problems. Slug bait should be set throughout the season in the confines of the greenhouse and cold frames, by scattering pellets under the staging and on the floor.

Outside, a little more attention to the location of the bait is necessary to prevent birds and pets eating the pellets. This is best achieved by placing the pellets in small quantities under a broken pot placed in such a position that there is only sufficient space for the slug or snail to enter. An alternative method is to set small shallow dishes filled with beer into the ground. Slugs cannot resist this beverage.

Mini slug pellets which contain metaldehyde, and are coated with a fungicide to give good weather resistance, are also repellent to animals and birds and a very effective slug bait.

Thrip

The adult flies are small and light brown, and commonly called 'thunder flies'. They extract sap from the leaves, buds and florets of the plant. The young wingless thrips are light green to yellow in colour, and feed on the undersides of leaves by piercing the epidermis and extracting sap.

Damage to young foliage by this pest results in the leaves having a mottled effect – the sap is extracted, and the leaf distorted as it grows. If the flower bud is attacked, the ends of the petals show a distinctive silvery effect, with white specks on the petals as they develop. Thrips can be especially damaging on deep colours such as red, bronze and purple. If the developing flower becomes infested, florets will wither and die.

Control of this type of pest is best achieved by using either 'Tumblebug', 'Sybol 2' or 'Rapid', while the plant is not showing colour. Freshly made 'Nico-Soap' can be sprayed on open blooms, providing it is a warm dull day. The blooms will not be affected.

Western Thrip

The amateur has not been too well informed about this relatively new species of thrip that is now becoming a problem to the commercial grower.

The insect is very much like the ordinary thrip and it is difficult to identify it from that species. The major difference is that the western thrip likes a warm atmosphere, such as the greenhouse, where it can lay its eggs in the ground. Attacks on outdoor cultivars have not been too many due to the cool weather conditions during the past few years, but damage to greenhouse-grown commercial crops has been on the increase. The eggs are laid in the soil of the greenhouse or pot plant, so spraying has to be carried out on a much more regular basis – possibly every two days – until the insect is eliminated. Insecticides for ordinary thrips should be used.

Vine Weevil

The vine weevil is commonly associated with pot plants and late-flowering chrysanthemums. As an adult it is black and wingless and feeds on the foliage. The eggs are normally transported into the greenhouse in loam and, on hatching out, the larva resembles a small white grub with a brown head and feeds on the roots and the stem below ground level. The adult insects are most prominent in late spring and early autumn.

Sterilisation of imported loam will reduce attacks of this pest, and fumigation with nicotine will kill off the insects. On occasions outdoor cultivars have been attacked. A top dressing of 'Bromophos' hoed into the top 1in (2.5cm) of soil will discourage the insect from laying its eggs, and normal spraying will deal with the adult insect.

White Fly

This is one of the most persistent insects to combat. It is not normally seen on outdoor cultivars, but it will spread to indoor cultivars from other host plants. It lays its eggs on the underside of leaves where both the larvae and adults feed. This insect has become immune to many insecticides and is difficult to control. Spraying should be carried out every three days until the infestation is killed off by using alternative insecticides – 'Nico-Soap', 'Malathion', 'Lindane' or 'Tumblebug'. Fumigation of the greenhouse should be done with nicotine shreads.

These pests can over-winter on weeds, so good hygiene is necessary to reduce an attack from this pest.

Wire Worms

These pests are often found in compost heaps constructed of turf. They are a hard yellow type of worm that feeds on the tips of roots and burrows into the stems of chrysanthemums. Unsterilised loam used in compost should be examined very carefully for this pest. Removal of weeds from the plot will greatly reduce the chances of an attack from this source, and 'Bromophos' sprinkled in the hole before planting is also a good deterrent.

Wood Lice

Wood lice are more of a nuisance than a serious threat to well-established plants in the greenhouse, but they will eat tender young shoots growing on stools in cold frames. The habit of these pests is to live in any decaying rubbish left lying around, so strict hygiene should be observed in the greenhouse and cold frames at all times. Dusting areas where they are known to hide with 'Nippon' will soon eradicate this pest.

PREDATORS

Every effort should be made to protect the few predators which are needed to keep these pests under control, and insecticides should only be used if predators are not present in large enough numbers. Before spraying I take a good look around the plants and remove all ladybirds to a safe area.

Ladybirds

These small beetles and their larvae are the natural enemy of aphids and will eat small infestations very quickly. There are three species: the seven-spotted, with a bright red coat and seven black spots; the two-spotted, with a bright red coat and a black spot on either side of its back; those with a black body with red patches on either shoulder. The larvae are approximately ½in (1.25cm) long, greyish in colour and can either have markings of red or yellow, or lines.

Hawkflies and Hover Flies

These two winged flies can be seen during warm summer days hovering above the plants. They lay their eggs amongst the aphids and as soon as they hatch out the larvae begin to feed on the aphids. It is reported that the larvae of the hawkfly can dispose of one hundred or more aphids in an hour.

Ichneumon Flies

Some ichneumon flies are similar to wasps in appearance, with slender bodies, and vary in size, from 1in (2.5cm) to as small as a midge. They have no sting but deposit their egg directly into the body of the victim which can be either an aphid or a caterpillar. The single egg then hatches out into a maggot that feeds on the body of its host.

Lace Wings

This fly is well named, for its slender body is supported by two pairs of lovely pale green wings that resemble fine lace. It is easily recognisable in flight. The female lays its eggs in groups on leaves – these can easily be mistaken for fungus growth. The larvae are a dirty white to brown in colour with brown or orange spots. Their main diet is aphids, and they will quickly devour a whole colony.

Spiders

The spider is another predator of the aphid and thrips, and should be encouraged in the chrysanthemum plot.

DISEASES

Crown Gall and Leafy Gall

Some cultivars seem to attract crown gall. It is a bacteria that attacks the base of the stem just below soil level, and is often not suspected during the growing season. Symptoms are irregular growths on the main stem just above the roots.

Leafy gall is a similar bacterial disease that deforms cutting material at the base of the stem. The cuttings are sometimes very thick, looking like two stems joined together, and the whole mass resembles the head of broccoli.

Both diseases are highly infectious and can be transmitted either in particles of soil or by hands that have been in contact with infected plants. The plant and surrounding soil should be burnt and if possible the ground sterilised.

Damping Off

This condition is associated with cuttings which often collapse and die off. This is caused by a fungus which attacks the stem below or at compost level, and decays the whole thing, turning it black. Bad management is often the culprit, providing ideal conditions for the fungus to attack either by over-watering, or by not making sure that the inserted part of the cutting is in contact with the compost throughout its entire length. If an air pocket is left between the end of the cutting and the bottom of the hole into which it is inserted, conditions will be ideal for an attack.

This disease is often transferred to the greenhouse in unsterilised loam, and warm conditions and insufficient ventilation will activate the disease. Watering with Chestnut Compound will give some protection.

Grey Mould (Botrytis)

This fungus is associated with poor ventilation, low temperatures, high humidity and damaged blooms. Greenhouses that are lined with polythene usually provide the ideal conditions for the disease.

The first indication of an attack is the appearance of small pink marks the size of a pin prick which spread rapidly, developing into dark brown, rotting patches. Sometimes a bruised or broken petal will cause the infection to start. The rotting area will soon become covered by a wet grey mould. If the bloom is shaken, the spores can be seen to drift in all directions: for this reason care must be taken when removing the infected bloom, and this must be done as soon as possible before healthy blooms also become infected. The best way to reduce the spread of spores is to inflate a large bag and put it over the diseased bloom, drawing the open end together and securing with a bag tie before cutting the bloom.

Grey mould is not only associated with open blooms but can be found on damaged leaves and young cuttings.

Spraying with a systemic fungicide during the season will build up a resistance. Late-flowering cultivars should be sprayed with a fungicide at both bud stage and just before housing. Fumigation of the greenhouse with smoke cones containing Lindane and Tecnazene (an ICI product) will help to control pests and botrytis.

The greenhouse should be well ventilated, and if the humidity in the greenhouse becomes high, the temperature should be increased. Watering pot plants should be carried out very sparingly, just sufficient to keep the plants topped up.

Foot and Stem Rot

The first indication of this disease is the lower leaves yellowing and dying. The plant growth is stunted, and gradually the yellowing leaves advance up the plant until the whole plant looks sick compared to its companions. Over-watering and poor drainage are the main causes, but it is also associated with composts with a high pH value. The disease is soil-borne and attacks the roots and stem of the plant causing both to rot and die.

If the plot has been infected with this disease, careful consideration should be given to improving the drainage, and before planting the area should either be sterilised or given a good watering with 'Zineb'. Pot-grown chrysanthemums that have contacted this disease should be burnt, together with the compost in which they were planted, and the pot thoroughly washed in a solution of 'Jeyes Fluid' and then rinsed in clear water.

Petal Blight

The first signs of an attack are similar to those of botrytis, but in this case the small spots are slightly more pink in colour when seen on light-coloured blooms. The spots quickly spread to form large wet areas which turn a dark brown as each petal becomes infected. The whole area rots and is susceptible to an attack of botrytis. In a short time the whole flower can become infected. The spores of this disease are very quickly spread in the greenhouse by electric fans, so the moment an infection is found you should switch off the fans and remove the infected bloom. Humidity in the greenhouse should be kept to a minimum, with windows and ventilators kept open during all favourable conditions, and gentle heat applied if the humidity begins to rise. Fumigation of the greenhouse with 'Fumite Tecnalin' smoke cones will give added protection.

Powdery Mildew

This disease is easily identified by grey powdery deposits found on many weeds and garden plants. The disease starts by attacking the underside of the lower leaves and, if unnoticed, spreads to the surface of the leaves, the stem and then the whole plant. It is often associated with lack of good ventilation in the greenhouse and long dry spells in the open.

Any lower infected leaves should be removed at once. On late-flowering cultivars you can remove all the leaves up to the break prior to housing, to improve air circulation around the plants and reduce the risk of attack.

With modern fungicides this disease is easy to control and providing fungicides have been used regularly there should be no problem. However, in case of an attack, spray with any of the following: 'Benlate', 'Tumbleblite' or 'Nimrod T'.

Ray Blight

This disease attacks the inner petals of maturing blooms and gradually spreads to the whole bloom. It is most active in heat and high humidity. The disease is incurable and the spores will spread to other flowers if they are not destroyed. Spraying with any of the above-mentioned fungicides and plenty of ventilation may prevent an attack.

Rust

This disease, which was practically unknown a few years ago, is beginning to reappear again. The first signs are yellowish spots on the surface of the leaf, and examination of the underside of the leaf will reveal brown blisters or pustules. If the blister is knocked the pustules will disperse in all directions so that the spores contaminate other plants in the area. Spores over-winter on stools and leaves that have not been collected up at the end of the season, so again hygiene is of the utmost importance. Hot water treatment will eradicate any spores that may be on the stools. In the case of a slight infection, the leaves should be removed from the plant and burnt. Badly infected plants should be destroyed and all surrounding plants should be sprayed on both sides of the leaves with 'Nimrod T'.

Verticillium Wilt

This fungal disease is found in garden soils, and when present may not attack some cultivars, but will be rampant on others. The disease spreads through the root system up the main stem, causing the foliage to turn yellow and hang limp. In some cases the infection is not noticed until flowering time, when the quality is found to be very poor. Some parts of the plant may be uninfected, whilst leaves on other laterals turn a reddish-brown and this colour change advances up the lateral. This colouring should not be mistaken for the effects of a cold night which will also discolour foliage. To check if the plant is infected, cut off the suspected lateral; if the centre of the stem is brown, this is a sure indication of the presence of verticillium wilt.

Control of this disease for the amateur is quite difficult, and the best remedy is to purchase new stock and use only sterilised loam for composts. If the plot is infected it should be sterilised, but if this is not practical, watering the area with a solution of 'Benlate' before planting and every ten days after planting will give some protection.

White Rust

Unfortunately, this disease has now become that widespread the Ministry of Agriculture, Fisheries and Food no longer requires notification. However, you should take every possible precaution to keep this disease to a minimum until the agrochemical companies can produce a fungicide to eradicate it. There are chemicals which will cure this disease but they are only available to professional nurserymen.

The disease first appears as small yellow dots on the surface of the leaves, and on inspection of the underside of the leaves small whitish-grey pustules will be seen. The pustules are transferred from one plant to another by wind or contact. It is estimated that spores can live and be transported on damp clothing for up to two hours from contact. High humidity helps the disease to spread, and it is known that spores will over-winter in the green tissue of the stem bark on stools.

Control, as already stated, is very difficult, but preventive measures can be taken. Spraying with 'Nimrod T' will give some protection and if an infection is found you should remove the infected plant and burn it. Spray all plants with 'Tumbleblite' at the rate of 1 fluid ounce per gallon (42ml per 4.5 litres) for the first spraying, and at ¾ fluid ounce (21ml per 4.5 litres) at 7-day intervals.

If an infection is found in the greenhouse, remove the infected plants and burn. Open all ventilators, keep the foliage dry and examine the other plants daily. If possible, take the plants out and spray them, as above, but be sure they are properly dry before rehousing.

Any new plants should be kept in isolation until you are satisfied that the new stock is clean.

If you are in any doubt seek advice.

Virus Diseases

There are many different types of viruses that can affect the chrysanthemum, but most of them are rare and many do not do too much harm. Some viruses are so minute that they cannot be identified by the human eye. There are a number of common ones that affect the chrysanthemum.

Asermy Virus

This virus deforms the flower and is the most common of all the viruses. The blooms are small and the colour of the bloom is not constant (this is totally different from a cultivar sporting). The colour of the petals within an infected bloom will show signs of streaking or be paler. In light-coloured blooms the virus is less evident, but the florets can be deformed. Usually the plant shows no sign of this infection until flowering time.

Virus B

This virus is not too harmful in chrysanthemums and is usually seen as yellow mottling on the leaves of young plants. As the plant develops the leaves revert to their normal colour. The virus appears to have no effect on the blooms themselves.

Stunt Virus

This is a serious virus which not only affects the growth of the plant, but also the quality of the blooms and the flowering time. The disease is usually carried from infected stock by sucking insects and secateurs and knives that have been used on infected plants.

Virus D and E

Often mistaken for aspermy virus but the loss of colour is not seen as streaks and more as lines or small blotches. Some of the developing florets fail to open, rendering the flower useless.

The only way an amateur can keep his stock relatively clear of viruses is by the following methods:

- Purchasing virus-free plants.
- Carrying out hot water treatment of the stools.
- Not propagating from stock that is suspect.
- Never using any implement (such as a knife or secateurs) to take cuttings, but breaking them off.
- Keeping to a strict spraying programme.
- Burning infected stock at once.

DISORDERS

Very often during the growing season plants are affected for no apparent reason, and explanations are hard to establish. Listed below are some of the unexpected problems I have experienced.

Blind Shoots

This is often caused by insect damage. Some cultivars are very susceptible to some insecticides, especially in the young stages of growth.

Chlorosis

Leaves turn a very pale green to whitish-green. This could be due to the following reasons:

- Deficiency in magnesium or manganese or both. Watering with a solution of Epsom Salts at the rate of 2oz per gallon (57g per 45 litres) will rectify this condition.
- Cold nights.
- The edges of young leaves changing to pale yellow is due to fumigating with nicotine. The plants will grow out of this condition.

Rotting Blooms

The florets in the centre of the bloom can turn black and start to rot. This is caused by excess feeds of nitrogen after the calyx has broken.

Stem Splitting

Some cultivars are prone to this disorder for no apparent reason, with buds literally popping off or snapping and bending over. Some growers associate this with climatic conditions, but I believe it is caused by too much water being available to the plant when the growing tip is very warm. This induces the sap to rise too quickly, which in turn causes the bud to pop.

If stems split vertically, again the cause seems to be the same. One thing common to both is that the neck below the bud shows signs of swelling. The build-up of sap can be relieved by pushing the blade of a penknife clean through the stem, forming a vertical cut to allow the sap to seep out.

Sun Scorch

The tips of the florets on one side of the bloom can turn brown and die, but this does not necessarily spread to the rest of the bloom. This is caused by the sun acting on moisture deposits on the petals – usually early-morning sunshine on overnight dew.

PLANT FOOD DEFICIENCY AND ITS EFFECTS

Most garden soils hold sufficient trace elements to provide the basic requirements for most of the plants grown in them, but these can become depleted if they are not replenished from time to time. In the case of plants grown in pots, the volume of soil available is limited and therefore more likely to show some form of deficiency. Plants grown in a soilless compost have to be provided with enough trace elements from the moment the compost is mixed. If a plot is used over a long period of time to grow one particular crop, the land will become out of balance, unless careful consideration is given to how and when chemical fertilisers are to be used. For this reason you should ensure careful monitoring of the contents of the soil, preferably on a yearly basis by soil testing.

Farmyard manures will provide some of the trace elements necessary, but this is too 'hit and miss' if your aim is to grow good quality blooms. Manure will not put the soil out of condition because the trace elements it contains are in such minute quantities, and the plant will only take exactly what it requires. The problems are caused when excessive amounts are applied without first ascertaining if they are needed. The amount of each trace element used by the plants varies – some are needed in such minute quantities they rarely ever show as a deficiency, while others are used in greater quantities and show any deficiency immediately. The latter are just as essential as nitrogen, potash and phosphates.

Problems arise when the phosphate, potash or pH levels become excessive, locking up the ingredients which the plant requires. Very little is known by the amateur grower of exactly how or in what proportions the plant uses these elements, but the keen gardener will soon become aware of any deficiency as his plants mature. Various trace elements are necessary to allow plants to make active roots and vegetative growth, and to create the ideal relationship between the pH of the soil and the elements themselves.

The ideal pH level for chrysanthemum growing in soil is 6.5, because at this level all the elements become available. The soil is slightly on the acid side, which allows elements such as boron, calcium, copper, iron, manganese, magnesium, phosphorus, nitrogen, potassium, sulphur and zinc to be made available to the plant. With a higher acid soil, with a pH of 5, only boron, copper, iron, manganese and possibly nitrogen would be available, and where the soil is high in alkaline, with a pH reading of 8, only calcium, magnesium, nitrogen and potassium would be available. If deficiencies do become a problem, therefore, you should first check the pH before applying additional elements.

There is an exception to this. Most soilless composts will show a pH reading of between 5.5 and 6. This is due to the acidity of the peat, and does not affect the elements required by chrysanthemums.

Boron

Deficiency is first apparent in the upper part of the plant and is indicated by the pale green leaves. This condition gradually spreads down the plant. If the deficiency is severe, the leaves become tough and turn downwards, while small younger leaves turn a pale yellow. Reflex blooms often have a number of petals that are tubular.

To combat this deficiency, apply a solution of borax at the

rate of 1oz (28.5g) dissolved in 4 gallons (18 litres) of water, giving each plant 1 pint (0.5 litre) twice a week until the symptoms improve.

Calcium

This element is necessary for the development of cell structure, and any deficiency is rapidly shown in the plant's health. The first indication is a slowing of the plant's growth, quickly followed by the roots dying. Leaves tend to take on a bluish-green appearance, and hang limp as though short of water. Give the area a liberal dressing of calcium carbonate at a rate of 4oz / sq yd (115g / sq m).

Copper

Plants grown in the garden seldom suffer from this deficiency because sufficient quantities of copper are present for the plants' requirements. Plants grown in soilless composts will show the symptoms of pale green areas between the veins of the leaves.

Treat the plants by spraying with a solution of copper sulphate at the rate of ¼oz (7g) dissolved in 4 gallons (18 litres) of water or by feeding the plants with a solution mixed at the rate of 1oz (28.5g) into 4 gallons (18 litres) of water, giving each plant 1 pint (0.5 litres).

Iron

This element is a vital ingredient in the formation of chlorophyll, and any deficiency soon becomes apparent by the leaves taking on a pale yellow appearance or (in the event of extreme deficiencies) an almost whitish look. The plant growth is retarded and soon the whole plant becomes very unhealthy. This condition can be rectified by applying sequestrene iron, which can be purchased at any garden centre. The crystals come in sachets and are dissolved into a prescribed amount of water and applied to the plant at the rate of 1 pint (0.5 litres) per plant once a week until the condition improves.

Magnesium

This element is a part of the chlorophyll in the leaf structure and symptoms of its deficiency are similar to those shown in iron deficiency. The main difference is that the veins stand out a deep green in a surrounding paleish yellow leaf. The ailment starts in the lower leaves first and gradually spreads to the whole plant.

Spray the plants with common agricultural Epsom Salts diluted at a rate of 1oz (28.5g) to 1 gallon (4.5 litres) of water, adding a few drops of washing-up liquid to prevent the solution running off the foliage too freely. Alternatively, dissolve 2oz (50g) of Epsom Salts into 1 gallon (4.5 litres) of water, and feed the plants with 1 pint (0.5 litres) of this solution each week until it shows signs of recovery.

Manganese

Again the symptoms are first noticed by the pale colour of the leaves, and the problem can easily be mistaken for magnesium deficiency. The difference is that the plant looks as though it has been grown in a partly-shaded area, having spindly laterals. The plant also becomes stunted with the leaves hanging down. Spraying will help in the early stages, but if the problem is not checked the plant will never produce first-class blooms. The spray solution should be made by dissolving 1oz (28.5g) of manganese sulphate into 4 gallons (18 litres) of water, and again adding a few drops of washing-up liquid to the solution.

Sulphur

A deficiency in this element is very difficult to identify because of the similarity to a deficiency in nitrogen. Symptoms are small leaves, stunted growth, and leaves showing signs of losing colour towards the bottom of the plant.

Sulphur deficiency was diagnosed in a soil test on one of my plots and I was told to treat the whole area with ½oz (14g) 'Flowers of Sulphur' per square yard (square metre).

THE IMPORTANT ELEMENTS

There are four major elements that provide the bulk of the plant's food which is necessary to form roots and vegetative growth. Without these elements the plant would die.

Calcium

Calcium is not only a plant food, needed to form the cell structure, but also acts as a soil conditioner.

Phosphorus

Phosphorus is of particular importance for encouraging the formation of good roots, but is not available in the soil in large quantities in a form that can be used by the plant. This is the reason that manure or some other form of organic matter is necessary – the bacteria works on the phosphorus and makes it available to the plant. A build-up of phosphorus (phosphate) in heavy soils can have a damaging effect on the growth of chrysanthemums. This element is also taken in by the roots and dispersed around the plant where it becomes available as required.

Symptoms of a deficiency are a reduction in the size of the leaves, followed by a slowing down of the plant's growth, until finally the plant ceases to develop. The foliage at this stage will have lost its green look, and will be dull and greyish.

A quick-acting fertiliser to use is 'Superphosphate' – 17–19 per cent P_2O_5 applied at the rate of 2–4oz (50–100g) per square yard (square metre) raked into the surface of the soil and watered in.

Occasionally there may occur the problem of excessive insoluble phosphates building up in the soil on a plot where you have grown chrysanthemums for many years. The plants become unable to use the phosphates and gradually the quality begins to deteriorate. In the end you have to remove all the soil from the whole plot and replace it with fresh. This usually happens because too much general fertiliser in powder form has been used as a top dressing. You should only use the recommended amount at planting time, and supplement feed with liquid fertiliser (which contains no phosphates) for the rest of the season.

Potassium

Potassium is used by the plant in large quantities for healthy and strong plant growth. It is a useful element to retard excess nitrogen uptake by the plant in a wet season. The level of potassium in light soils tends to be on the low side because of the structure of the soil, whereas heavy clay soils seem to retain the element over a longer period.

Deficiency of this element is indicated by the lower leaves turning yellow and then brown. In severe cases the leaves start to die from the base upwards. To combat this deficiency the plant should be watered with a solution of 1oz (28.5g) of sulphate of potash 50 per cent K_2O dissolved in 5 gallons (22.5 litres) of water every other watering. Alternatively, use 'Chempak No. 10' liquid fertiliser which has a ratio of 3–1 potash to nitrogen, and give each plant 1 pint (0.5 litre) at each watering until the plant starts to improve.

Nitrogen

This element is very important in a number of ways. It is found in the leaves to form chlorophyll, and is the basic ingredient for forming cell structure and the growth of the plant. Therefore, any reduction of this element soon becomes apparent. Normally this element is in reasonable quantities at the start of the season, mainly because the plant is small and preoccupied with forming roots, but as the plant starts to grow so does its appetite for nitrogen. At this stage it should be given liquid supplementary feeds of equal parts nitrogen and potash. The emphasis should be to keep the plant moving without over-feeding with nitrogen, otherwise the plant will be too soft with tough and bloated leaves of a very dark green. These will be of little use later for producing the much-needed sugars for feeding the bloom. Nitrogen deficiency is apparent when the leaves tend to turn a pale green and the growth slows down. In severe cases the leaves are small and may show signs of discoloration in shades of red and purple (this should not be mistaken for the effect of cold nights on old leaves).

Liquid feeding of high nitrogen will soon improve any deficiency. The plants should be given alternative waterings of a solution of 1oz (28.5g) sulphate of ammonia dissolved into 4 gallons (18 litres) of water. Each plant should be given 1 pint (0.5 litre) at each watering until the plant shows signs of recovery. Alternatively, give a liquid feed with 'Chempak No.9', which has a ratio of 3–1 nitrogen to potash.

Air

Air is rarely mentioned when plant foods are discussed and yet is vitally important. The roots of the plant need access to air to develop and grow, and an active root system is the result of a combination of air, plant food and moisture. Any compost or soil must, therefore, be of a type that allows air and moisture to be retained within its structure. There should be a sufficient quantity of each for the plant's requirements, but the moisture should not be so much as to exclude the air completely.

Deficiency of this ingredient is not normally a problem, unless the compost has become waterlogged due to insufficient drainage. The symptoms of waterlogging are leaves becoming yellow and the vigour of the plant slowing down until it finally stops. The surface area of the compost is always wet and on examination the roots are found to be dark brown and dead. If the problem is diagnosed early it is possible to re-pot the plant and it will then produce a new root system. If it goes undetected the whole plant will die.

11

New Cultivars

SPORTING

Some growers have the good luck to have more than one cultivar sport, while others will never have it happen. This process of 'sporting' is interesting to the gardener. A new chrysanthemum first starts life when pollen is transferred from one plant to another. This is transported into the ovary of the stamen where it is fertilised to form a seed. The seed will have chromosomes from both parents, and as it develops and the cells divide the chromosomes split and multiply. Chrysanthemums can have anything from 45 to over 100 chromosomes, and each chromosome has several hundred genes. It is these genes that determine the characteristics of the plant – its height, colour, size of foliage and vigour. If the developing plant is always in a stage of splitting cells, there comes a point when the genes are not in the same order, resulting in a physical change in the plant. Some of these changes are so small that they go unnoticed, but occasionally the colour of the bloom will show signs of the change. It can vary from just one single petal to a whole bloom, and involve slightly different colour or a totally different colour. In some cases a quarter of the bloom is completely different from the rest of the bloom.

When the whole bloom or the biggest part of the bloom has sported, there is more chance of the amateur securing the sport. In the case of a few single petals it is more complex and laboratory conditions are necessary.

Securing a Sport

If the whole bloom on one lateral is a new sport, there are two ways of obtaining plants identical to the sport:

(i) Remove all other laterals, including the flowering head of the sport, and allow all the side shoots to grow from that lateral. When they are about 2in (5cm) long, remove them from the stem and treat as cuttings. Remember not to take any cutting material from below the break of the main plant. (ii) Prepare the lateral as above, but cut short horizontal nicks in the stem of the lateral just below a leaf joint. Bend the whole plant over and peg the lateral into the ground, making sure each cut in the stem is in contact with the ground. Soil is then placed on the stem of the lateral between each leaf axil joint. Roots will grow from these cuts to form a complete plant. The disadvantage of this method is that there could be insufficient time to allow the lateral to root. In this case it would be better to prepare the lateral as described and then lift the plant, place in a large pot and take it into the greenhouse. Cut half the lateral off and divide up into sections, with each section having a leaf joint with a small section of stem. Place these in a rooting tray in a propagator and treat as cuttings. Allow the other section of the lateral to remain on the old plant, and secure any cuttings that grow from the lateral.

Securing sports from blooms where only a portion of the bloom is affected is more difficult, and although plants may be rooted there is always a chance that many will reproduce the old cultivar. Nevertheless, it is always worth a try.

Unlike the full sport, only a section of the lateral from the point of flowering down to the break will have mutated, and even this may not necessarily cover the full length of the lateral. It could be just a short length below the bloom, and the width of the mutation down the lateral may be very narrow. In this case the bloom should not be removed until the lateral has been prepared.

First look at the lateral, and imagine a straight line drawn from the section of the bloom which has sported straight down the lateral to the break. Any leaf joints on this line are a possible source of new plants of the sport, but remember the leaf joints must be coming from the lateral immediately on the line. Leaf joints on either side of the line are unlikely to be successful and should be removed, together with leaf joints on the opposite side of the lateral. The prepared lateral should show a line of leaf joints descending from the bloom head, along the imaginary line down to the break, with all other vegetative growth removed. At this point the flower head can be removed. As explained above, side shoots are allowed to grow from these leaf joints and then rooted as cuttings. All other growth should be removed as soon as possible to direct all energy into producing side shoots.

Another method is to remove the lateral from the plant after it has been prepared as above, then cut it into sections long enough to fit on to the top of a seed tray that has been filled with a rooting medium. Then, on the opposite side of each leaf joint, cut half-way through the lateral, peg the cut side down on to the rooting mediuma and place in the propagator. This will encourage the side shoots to grow quickly and roots to form in the cut section. Once plants have been obtained with a good root system, the top section of the plant with a pair of leaves should be taken as a cutting and rooted again. This will not only increase the stock but also the chances of securing the sport.

Where only a few petals are a different colour from the rest of the bloom a new sport can be grown under laboratory conditions. The bloom is collected from the garden and taken to a laboratory, where the different petals are removed and sterilised. The petals are treated and allowed to callous over, then placed in a test tube on a bed of nutrients. Small shoots develop and cuttings are taken and grown into plants.

White cultivars on occasions will naturally sport to pink, bronze and yellow, and deep-coloured cultivars will sport through a range of colours, but yellow cultivars only sport to white or a deeper yellow. Where a white cultivar has sported to yellow it is not unusual for that sport to revert back to white at some stage. Sports from pink cultivars are regarded as the best, because there is a good chance they will produce other coloured sports.

Induced sports

Experiments have been carried out with chrysanthemum plants and cuttings which have been subjected to a bombardment of gamma rays or X-rays. The effect has been to bring about changes to the cell structure of the plant more quickly, resulting in many new sports. Commercial nurserymen have used this facility on cultivars that have proved to be very good in the cut flower trade, especially late-flowering sprays. However, some of the sports were not stable and reverted back to the original colour.

BREEDING

The process of breeding new cultivars has been carried out since the first cultivars were introduced into the UK. Each year hundreds of new seedlings are produced, and many are discarded before the general public have a chance to see them. One well-known nurseryman grows as many as a thousand seedlings each year; only a handful will be selected for growing on the following year, and then selection will reduce the number even more, until final release, which could be as long as four or even five years from the time the seed was first planted. Hence the high cost of new cultivars.

Nurserymen are reluctant to reveal the breeding lines of the parents of a good cultivar, but the following will help you in selecting parents for cross-pollination to produce cultivars for exhibition, cut flower trade and general garden decoration. Exhibition cultivars will have to conform to the standards laid down for a particular section, so you should be looking for parents that have form, strong stems, quality and good colour, are not too soft, are reliable, and disease free.

For commercial purposes the breeding line would be slightly different, as the emphasis would be on producing a better bloom than was already available – an attractive colour or a multi-coloured type, or an eye-catching bloom on a strong long stem that will crop well. Cultivars for the garden would need to be weather resistant and not too tall, have strong stems, be early flowering, crop well and resist disease.

The technique of crossing two chrysanthemums is not simple, but the challenge is well worth the effort. The following notes can only give the general principles, and I recommend you read the booklet *Chrysanthemum Breeding* by G. Wilson (published by the NCS).

Getting Started

Selection of parents should be made from good healthy stock, and, for the first-time hybridiser, from the same section – reflexes with reflexes, larges with larges and so on. Experiments can be done later with different sections once the initial experience has been gained. Colour crosses are quite acceptable but you should bear in mind that there is no guarantee that the colour produced will resemble that of either parent. The next step is to prepare each cultivar for producing and receiving the pollen.

Cultivars that are selected for producing pollen should be grown in a compost with very little nutritional value, and only given water to keep them alive. Plants can be stopped either in early May and again in early July, or just once in May. All laterals are allowed to flower, to encourage the plant to produce blooms with very few petals and show a daisy eye similar to the bloom of a single cultivar. For this purpose it is better to plant two or three plants of the same cultivar in 5in (12.5cm) pots, or even closer together in the open garden. The cultivar that will become the seed bearer should be grown in compost that should have a little more fertiliser, but should not be too rich. This will encourage more petals, and the plant should be given two or three high potash feeds as soon as the petals begin to show colour, to make sure that the stem is ripe and not soft and green.

Some nurserymen grow the selected cultivars for crossing in pots in a greenhouse where they have a much tighter control of temperatures and humidity. However, for the beginner early-flowering cultivars are fine to begin with, as pollen is much easier to obtain in August and September.

Preparing the Blooms

Blooms that are selected as pollen bearers should be cut from the plant, with a stem about 15in (37.5cm) long, when they are fully developed. The foliage is removed from the stem and any disc and all the ray florets are gently pulled out to reveal the receptacle (flower head) (see diagram opposite).

The blooms of the cultivar selected for seed bearing should be cut from the plant, with a stem about 15in (37.5cm) long, when the blooms are roughly half developed. Again, all the foliage is removed, then, with the bloom held upside down, the ray florets are cut off with a sharp razor blade. Gently work around the bloom head, cutting until the style in the petal is just visible below where the petal has been cut off. All the disc florets should then be gently pulled out (see diagram overleaf.). It may be necessary to repeat this task several times over a few days before the style is near to the surface where the upper section of the petal has been removed.

As each cultivar is prepared it should be placed in a glass jar or vase half-filled with water with disinfectant added. Crystals can be obtained from florists, or mix ½ teaspoonful of Milton with ½ teaspoonful of alum into 4 pints (2.25

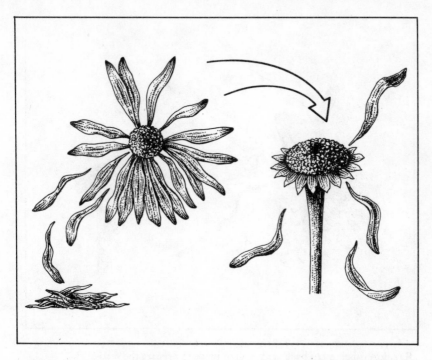

Ray florets being removed from the flowering head that will provide the pollen.

litres) of water. Label the jars with the name of the cultivar and whether it is a seed bearer or pollen bearer, and then place them in a fairly dry atmosphere, such as a shelf above a radiator, to allow the staminal tube to extend so that ripe pollen is available. As this happens, small grains become visible on the staminal and the smell of the pollen is also an indication. A watch should be kept on the water level in the containers and it should be changed weekly.

Pollen may be ready before the stigma of the ray florets are sufficiently extended to accept it, so you, may have to collect the pollen and store it. Use a small glass jar with a screw top that has been washed out and dried (fish paste jars are ideal). Into the jar place a few crystals of silica gel and cover with cotton wool. The pollen is collected by means of an artist's paintbrush and placed either in a small greaseproof bag, or on greaseproof paper, which is then folded and sealed with sticky tape. The packet is put into the sealed jar and kept in a cool dry place.

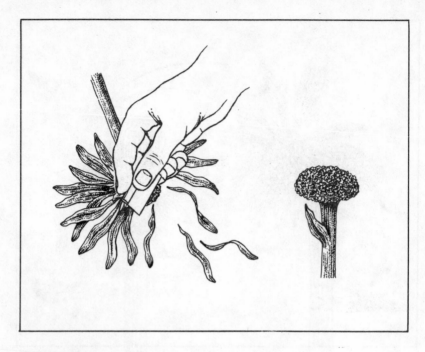

Ray florets being cut back with a razor blade to prepare the seed-bearing head.

Pollination

As soon as the stigma (commonly referred to as the 'antlers' of the style) is elongated above the cut section of the petal base, pollination can begin. Pollen is transferred from the pollen-bearing flower head with either an artist's brush or the head of an unused matchstick, and is gently pushed into the stigmas to prevent it being dislodged or knocked off. Some hybridisers regard the use of a match unsuitable, as this can damage the tender stigmas if sufficient care is not taken. The pollination of the seed-bearing flower head should be repeated two or three times on the same stigmas over a period of a week, to ensure that each one has been successfully treated. Some breeders use a magnifying glass to enable them to direct the small grains of pollen into the stigma. This method is extremely useful when insufficient pollen is available.

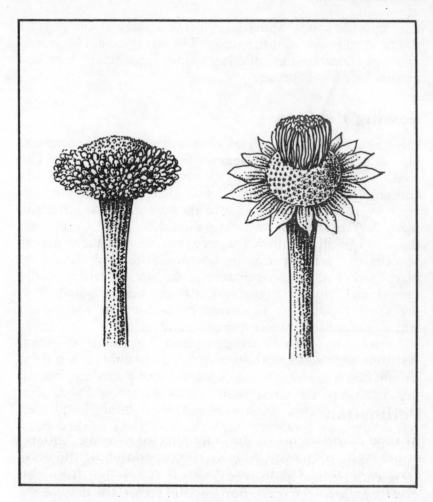

(Left) Seed-bearing head with ray florets cut back. (Right) Flower head showing disc florets ready to produce pollen.

Collecting the Seeds

The water level in the containers should be maintained after fertilisation until the seed head has fully ripened. Some breeders cover the seed-bearing head with a brown paper bag drawn together at the open end and tied securely around the stem. It will take anything from 8 to 12 weeks for the seeds to ripen and be ready for collection. The head will go brown and very dry, falling to bits if gently rubbed in the hands. When the seed head has ripened it should be removed from the stem. A sheet of brown paper is spread out on a table and the seed head is gentle tapped, allowing the seeds to fall on to the paper. Sometimes it is necessary to disintegrate the head to recover all the seeds. The seeds should be stored in a dry container until the right time for sowing, which is usually in early February.

Sowing the Seed

It is essential to use sterilised loam in the planting compost, but, as with rooting cuttings, no fertiliser is necessary. The seeds should be sown very thinly on the surface of the compost and lightly covered with sharp or silver sand. A light overhead watering should then be given to settle the seeds in. Any further watering should be given by placing the seed tray in a shallow tray of water, so that the compost absorbs the water from the bottom. The tray should be placed either in the propagator, or on heating cables on the open bench alongside cuttings that are being rooted. It is necessary to observe the same precautions as for rooted cuttings regarding air temperature and light.

Germination can take anything from 3 weeks to 10 weeks. As each new seedling becomes large enough to handle it should be removed from the seed tray and potted on, but do not dispose of the compost in the seed tray until well after the 10-week period. First-year seedlings should be planted out as for early-flowering cultivars, all in the same bed and a little closer together than for exhibition blooms. As a general guide, stop all the plants in early May, providing they are large enough, and allow 4 to 5 breaks to develop. Give each plant a code or reference number and record the date of the stop and everything relating to the plant.

First-year seedlings are very vigorous in growth so there should be no need to supplement the base dressing with liquid feeds. The treatment of the blooms should be as already described for cut flowers, sprays and exhibition, whichever cultivars were used for the breeding programme.

The seedlings can be a mixed bag, containing anything from reflexes to incurves and in any shade of colour. It is therefore important that only the best seedlings are retained for further trials as second-year seedlings, and any that do not come up to scratch are burnt. Next year's cuttings can be taken from the selected stools, as described for other cultivars.

REGISTRATION AND CLASSIFICATION

There are two sources for registration of chrysanthemums in the United Kingdom – the Plant Breeders' Rights Office, and the National Chrysanthemum Society.

Plant Breeders' Rights

The above was set up under the Plant Varieties and Seed Act 1964 to administer Part 1 of that Act.

If a raiser of a new cultivar wishes, he can register the cultivar with the Plant Breeders' Rights Office, which is a form of patent, and no one can reproduce that cultivar for resale without first obtaining a licence to do so. This service is used by the commercial trade to protect their new cultivars, after they have spent many years and large investments on their breeding programme. The raiser applies to the Plant Breeders' Rights Office at Whitehouse Lane, Huntingdon Road, Cambridge CB3 0LF, and all the relative information concerning the new cultivar is submitted together with the chosen name and registration fee. The application is vetted by the Controller who has to satisfy himself that the cultivar is distinct, stable and uniform. When all these points have been checked, he will decide whether or not to grant Plant Breeders' Rights to the raiser of the cultivar.

This form of registration is to protect the commercial raisers from exploitation by other nurserymen. Registrations under this scheme are purely for commercial cultivars and are not eligible for exhibition under NCS rules.

National Chrysanthemum Society

There are cultivars that have been granted 'Rights' which are also eligible for exhibition, having been classified and registered by the Joint Floral Committee of the Royal Horticultural and National Chrysanthemum Societies. For example, the late-flowering cultivar 'Satin Pink Gin' is subject to plant breeders' rights, but, because it was such a good quality late-flowering spray, a top exhibitor obtained permission for it to be registered, and it was classified as 9c LP and can now be exhibited. (Stock of that cultivar can only be obtained from those who have been given permission to reproduce it.)

The National Chrysanthemum Society Floral Committee

is the national body responsible for the classification of all new chrysanthemums and sports (that are sufficiently distinct from their parents) to be registered in the UK. It consists of eighteen Fellows and a Chairman elected by the National Chrysanthemum Society Executive Committee, plus three *ex-officio* members.

The Joint Chrysanthemum Committee consider cultivars for awards and make recommendations to both the RHS and the NCS. The committee consists of eighteen members, nine appointed by the RHS and nine appointed by the NCS. The Chairman is elected each year on an alternating basis by the RHS and the NCS. Meetings are arranged and publicised by both the RHS and the NCS for the purpose of classification and recommending awards. The meetings are held in the south of the UK at the RHS Gardens at Wisley and at the National Shows in London, and in the north of the UK at Harrogate.

Where registration and classification have been arranged in conjunction with a national or group show, the new cultivars are displayed to the general public. New cultivars registered at Wisley are not normally put on display, but it is hoped to rectify this in the future.

Registration

Any cultivar that is not shown in the National Chrysanthemum Register can be submitted to the Joint Floral Committee for registration and classification at any of their meetings by any person, whether a raiser or not. Application forms can be obtained from the Secretary of the National Chrysanthemum Society, and this should be completed and brought with the appropriate blooms to the meeting. When applying for registration forms it is necessary to inform the Secretary of the proposed name chosen for the new cultivar, so that he can check that it is acceptable.

Cultivars that are to be put before the Joint Floral Committee should be grown to their best possible standard, and should not be submitted if the blooms are too young or too old. It is far better to submit the blooms at a later meeting than to be told the blooms are not worthy of registration. In some cases the committee will register the name only and defer classification until the blooms are seen in better condition. The registration form gives details of the number of blooms required for registration purposes: large and medium exhibition cultivars need one bloom only, while pot plants need one pot only. For awards, three blooms with foliage are required for all sections, except in the case of pot plants where only one pot is required, and spray cultivars where three stems of sprays are required.

Sports can only be registered if the sport has been inspected growing by a member of the floral committee. Three blooms of the sport will be required, plus one bloom from the cultivar it has sported from, together with a bloom of any similar coloured sport of that cultivar. Sports are not eligible for consideration for an award during the first year of their exhibition.

Classification

Because of the many different types and forms of chrysanthemums it has been necessary to segregate them into six groups:

- Incurve
- Reflex
- Intermediate
- Anemone
- Pompon
- Single
- Spray

Each cultivar is allocated a section number which indicates when the cultivar will be in full bloom, if it is grown naturally in a normal season.

Cultivars that flower from November onwards are given section numbers from 1 to 12. Cultivars that flower from early October to November are given section numbers 13 to 20, and cultivars that flower before October are placed in sections 22 to 30.

LATE-FLOWERING CULTIVARS

Section 1	Large exhibition blooms
Section 2	Medium exhibition blooms (this is the only section allocated to medium blooms)
Section 3	Incurved
Section 4	Reflexed
Section 5	Intermediate
Section 6	Anemones

Section 7   Singles
Section 8   Pompons

(Sections 3 to 8 have three sub-sections to distinguish the size
of the bloom: (a) large, (b) medium and (c) small.)

Section 9   Sprays
(This section contains six sub-sections to accommodate the
different types of blooms within this section: (a) anemones,
(b) pompons, (c) reflexed, (d) singles, (e) intermediate, and
(f) spiders, quills, spoons (single or double) and any other
type.)
Section 10   (a) Spiders, (b) Quills, (c) Spoons
Section 11   Any other types
Section 12   (a) Charms
               (b) Cascades

October-Flowering Cultivars
Section 13   Incurved
Section 14   Reflexed
Section 15   Intermediate
Section 16   Large October-flowering
Section 17   Singles
Section 18   Pompons
               (a) True pompons
               (b) Semi-pompons
Section 19   Sprays.
(With the same sub-sections as for late-flowering sprays.)
Section 20   Any other types
(Sections 13 to 17 have three sub-sections: (a) large, (b)
medium, and (c) small.)

EARLY-FLOWERING CHRYSANTHEMUMS –
OUTDOOR CULTIVARS
Section 22   Charms
Section 23   Incurved
Section 24   Reflexed
Section 25   Intermediate
Section 26   Anemones
               (a) Large-flowered
               (b) Medium-flowered

Section 27   Singles
                    (a) Large-flowered
                    (b) Medium-flowered
Section 28   Pompons
                    (a) True-pompons
                    (b) Semi-pompons
Section 29   Sprays
(With the same sub-sections as before.)
Section 30   Any other type
(Sections 23 to 25 all have three sub-sections: (a) large, (b) medium, and (c) small.)

The colours of the blooms are also classified, according to the National Chrysanthemum colour charts, which allow all blooms to be given a key code which precedes the classification. There are 21 colours, as follows:

W	White	LB	Light bronze
Cr	Cream	B	Bronze
LY	Light yellow	DB	Deep bronze
Y	Yellow	LR	Light red
DY	Deep yellow	R	Red
LP	Light pink	DR	Deep red
P	Pink	LPu	Light purple
DP	Deep pink	Pu	Purple
LS	Light salmon	DPu	Deep purple
S	Salmon	OC	Other colours (green, etc)
DS	Deep salmon		

When blooms are submitted before the Joint Floral Committee, the submitter should arrange to arrive at the venue at least one hour before the meeting is scheduled to start, to enable the RHS and NCS Secretaries to have the paperwork completed in readiness for the meeting. Vases are provided at the meeting, and when the blooms have been staged an assistant will place a card in front of the vase of blooms indicating what classification and colour the raiser recommends for registration, and the proposed name. This card will remain with the blooms during the meeting and any alteration to classification will be recorded on the card, together with any proposed award.

There are a few stipulations regarding the naming of blooms:

(i)   The name of a new cultivar should not exceed two

words, with the exception of sports, when three words may be used.

(ii) The name cannot be prefixed with Mr, Miss or any such abbreviations. A person's name must be in full.

(iii) If the raiser or submitter wishes to name the cultivar after a particular person, they should first obtain the person's permission to use his or her name.

(iv) Long and difficult names should be avoided.

(v) Names that are in the register may be re-used, providing the original stock is extinct, but not if the registered cultivar was given an RHS award.

(vi) All sports must bear the name of the parent cultivar they sported from. For example 'Venice' sporting salmon would be registered 'Salmon Venice'.

Procedure

The Chairman reads out the information from the application form as each vase of blooms is presented to the members to examine. When every member has had the opportunity to look at the blooms the Chairman will call on them first to agree the classification. The members of this committee are vastly experienced, and very often will identify a cultivar not seen for years. Their examination will tell them if the bloom is worthy of registration, in which section it belongs, and also whether it is a large, medium or small bloom. The next step is to agree the colour. If there is any doubt as to which shade of colour is correct, the colour charts are used and shades compared. If the cultivar is a new seedling it can be proposed by one of the members for an award, and, if seconded, the matter would then be put to a vote.

There are four categories for awards:

● Exhibition, denoted by the letter 'E' after the award.
● Cut flower, denoted by the letter 'C' after the award.
● Pot plants, denoted by the letter 'P' after the award.
● Garden decoration, denoted by the letter 'G' after the award.

A cultivar may be registered as either an exhibition or cut flower and can be proposed for a PC, but a cultivar that is registered for garden decoration cannot be considered until it has been selected for trials, and then it can be recommended for an award when seen growing in the ground.

Preliminary Commendation

An award of 'preliminary commendation' can be recommended for exhibition, cut flower or pot plant cultivars at the time they are submitted for registration, or at any other time in the future. The proposal to make such an award must obtain double the votes in favour to those against.

Sports are not eligible for consideration unless they were registered in the previous season.

Cultivars registered may be considered for trials. If a cultivar is considered worthy for trials the raiser will be asked to provide a certain number of plants to be grown at both the RHS Gardens, Wisley, and at the trial grounds in northern Britain. The Floral Committee makes regular visits to both trials, and inspects the cultivars at flowering time. It is at these inspections that the committee will make their recommendation for awards, based on whether the flowers are weather resistant, produce a good display of blooms, have good colour and healthy foliage, and are of reasonable height.

Cultivars that were registered and recommended for a PC award will have the award shown after the classification in the National Chrysanthemum Register, together with the year in which it was registered. For example, 'Mancetta Pearl' is shown in the register as follows:

'Mancetta Pearl' (G. Freestone) 1987 4b OC PC/E

This means the cultivar was raised by Mr G. Freestone and submitted for registration in 1987, and was awarded a Preliminary Commendation for Exhibition.

Award of Merit

When a cultivar has received a PC it can be submitted at another meeting to be considered for an Award of Merit. A cultivar being submitted for this award must be at its peak and a perfect specimen of that section. The voting procedure is exactly the same as for a PC.

First-Class Certificate

This award can only be made to a cultivar that has already received an Award of Merit, and has been released and been in general cultivation for at least one year. The voting for this award must be 3 to 1 in favour.

Highly Commended

This is an award for cultivars grown in the open ground. The number of cultivars under trials at one time may vary from 150 to 190, covering all aspects of early-flowering chrysanthemums. The cultivars are grown in groups of twelve plants of the same cultivar. Each group has a display notice indicating when the plants were stopped, and whether the cultivar has been given an award.

Many cultivars that are selected may remain in the trials for many years. Some receive an award of HC/G in the first year, and eventually AM and FCC. If a cultivar has not received an award at the end of three years, it is deleted from the trials.

For a cultivar to receive an award for garden decoration the voting must be 2 to 1 in favour for either an HC or AM, and 3 to 1 for an FCC.

It is well worth paying a visit to the RHS Gardens at Wisley during the period August to October to see the many types of chrysanthemums under trials in the open ground. During November a demonstration of late-flowering sprays, charms, and cascades can be seen in the greenhouse.

12

Plant Lists

CULTIVARS SUITABLE FOR GARDEN DECORATION OR CUTTING

Disbuds

Angora 25b O   This is a relatively old cultivar that has stood the test of time. Registered in 1975, it received an FCC in 1984 and still remains in the RHS and NCS trials. The blooms are of incurving form in a delicate shade of salmon pink. Fairly weather-resistant and grows to a height of 42in (105cm).

Alouise 25b LP   Another well-tried cultivar of the same form as 'Angora', which has sported bronze, yellow, salmon and white. Registered in 1976.

Autumn Days 25b B   This is a semi-incurving bronze with the petals showing a gold reverse. Was awarded an HC in trials in 1978.

Bessie Rowe 25a W   A pure white incurving type that does well outdoors.

Betty Wiggins 25a Y   Large incurving type with rich, golden-yellow blooms. The plant is short and sturdy, growing to a height of 30in (75cm).

Cricket 25b W   This has a hard open-type petal structure that stands up to the weather. It grows to a height of 42in (105cm). There are two sports of this cultivar, primrose and yellow, both with the same characteristics of the parent.

Early Bird 24b Pu   This is a spiky light purple reflex that flowers very early. There are two sports of this cultivar in red and rose-pink.

Eve Gray 24b P A lovely pink reflex cultivar that will stand up to the weather. It grows to a height of 42in (105cm).

Foxdown 25b B A chestnut bronze of incurving form that flowers at 48in (120cm).

Gazelle 23a W A lovely white incurve with a fine petal structure that seems to glisten. Height 48in (120cm).

Hazel Zwager 24b P This salmon pink reflexing cultivar is very weather-resistant and will give excellent results outdoors. There are two sports of this cultivar in bronze and a ruby-wine colour.

Joyce Stevenson 24b R A very good cultivar that will stand up to the rain and wind when grown in the open for cutting. The blooms are a deep red in colour, with petals that reflex straight back to the stem. This cultivar is still shown as an exhibition variety. Height is 48in (120cm).

June Wakeley 25b LP A rose-pink intermediate that is ideal for cutting or garden decoration.

Regalia 24b Pu This reflex is as hard as nails when exposed to the weather. The petals stand out at right angles to the stem and are purple in colour with a lighter shade underneath. It flowers from August onwards at a height of 42in (105cm).

Verona 15b Pu This is a cultivar that blooms in late September, of tight incurving form and very weather-resistant. An ideal cut flower. Height 48in (120cm).

Early-flowering Pompons

These delightful cultivars produce a mass of perfectly-shaped balls of florets on plants varying from 16in (40cm) to 28in (70cm) tall and are ideal for a border or bedding work.

Bright Eye A brilliant yellow with a red centre. Height 28in (70cm).

Cameo A pure white. Height 22in (55cm).

Denise   A clear yellow. Height 16in (40cm).

Fairie   A lovely pink. Height 16in (40cm). There are four sports of this cultivar in bronze, purple, salmon and yellow.

Jane Wells   A very old cultivar that has stood the test of time. This cultivar produces a mass of lovely yellow blooms. Height 15in (37.5cm).

Mavis   A pink with a very attractive dark centre. Height 18in (45cm).

Solley   Lemon in colour with a distinctive golden centre. Height 18in (45cm).

Otley Koreans and Rubellums

These delightful cultivars were very popular in the 1950s and 1960s and are once more coming back into favour. They are ideal for filling up an odd spot in a herbaceous border to give that added touch of colour in September and also very useful for floral art work or for display as pot plants for the patio. They will grow in the shade but this tends to delay the blooms coming into flower. These cultivars come in a wide range of colours and vary in height from 12in (30cm) to 30in (75cm).

Otley Koreans

Agnes Ann   This is a double-flower type of bloom of a deep red velvet colour, and flowers at a height of 15in (37.5cm).

Aunt Millicent   The flowers are of a silvery-pink with a yellow centre. Height 20in (50cm).

Fairy Rose   A rose-pink single that produces an abundance of lovely blooms. Suitable for use as a pot plant. Height 18in (45cm).

Raquel   A lovely mauve/pink single with a yellow disc. The plant is of a bushy habit that has masses of lovely blooms. Height 15in (37.5cm).

Rubellums

Alberts Yellow   A brilliant yellow single that is ideal for cutting and for floral art work. Height 18in (45cm).

Duchess of Edinburgh   A deep copper-red single with a lovely yellow disc that makes this a very attractive flower. Height 30in (75cm).

Mary Stoker   This cultivar with its very unusual colour of creamy yellow-apricot has very attractive single flowers. Height 24in (60cm).

Nell Gwynn   A pink single with a yellow circle around the base of the petals which makes the whole bloom stand out. The blooms are ideal for flower arranging and cutting. Height 18in (45cm).

Ruby Raynor   This is a double bloom of a rich golden colour and is ideal for use as a cut flower. Height 30in (75cm).

American Cushion Mums

These new early charm chrysanthemums come in a wide range of colours and give masses of blooms from early August to well into October.

Debonair   Will produce a bush plant 18in (45cm) in diameter with a mass of delightful rose-pink double flowers. Height 12in (30cm).

Encore   A white double-flowering cultivar which, like all these charms, develops into a bushy plant covered with blooms. Height 15in (37.5cm).

Ginger   The double bronze flowers are almost perfect balls which form a nice neat bushy plant. Height 18in (45cm).

Goldmine   This is a yellow with blooms not quite as large as 'Debonair', but nevertheless a delightful plant. Height 15in (37.5cm).

Grenadine   This salmon-coloured double-flowering cultivar is a very attractive plant. Height 12in (30cm).

Remarkable   The flowers are a lovely shade of red that do
not seem to fade even in full sunlight. Height 12in (30cm).

There are many more Cushion Mums in addition to those
mentioned and all are equally as good. To prolong the
flowering period, all dead blooms should be removed and
the plants given a liquid feed every week.

Garden Charms

There are several garden charms on the market which are
suitable for displaying on patios as pot plants or garden
borders. The following are the single-bloom type which
grow to a height of 12in (30cm). Each plant produces
hundreds of small star-like single flowers with yellow discs.

Redwings, Wagtail (white), **Goldcrest, Skylark** (peach),
and **Chaffinch** (the blooms on this cultivar have petals
varying from a delicate shade of pink to a very deep pink).

Chrysanthemum Frutescens

With their fern-like foliage, these are ideal as a ground-
covering decorative plant or for cut blooms for floral art.
There are two types – anemone-centred and singles. Singles
come in two colours (white and yellow), anemone in pink.

Early-Flowering Garden Sprays

There are so many to choose from that I have only listed
some of the cultivars that have produced plenty of blooms
and have proved to be reliable over many years.

Cultivars Flowering August / September

Anna Marie   A pure white cultivar that flowers from early
August. Height 36in (90cm).

Broadway Mandy   Salmon-pink double flower. Height
42in (105cm).

Dee Lemon As the name indicates, a lovely shade of lemon, with double flowers. This cultivar is of dwarf habit. Height 36in (90cm).

Gerrie Hoek A deep rose-pink. Height 36in (90cm).

Jenny Orange-bronze. Height 42in (105cm).

Lilian Hoek Bright orange double flowers. Height 36in (90cm). There are other sports of this cultivar that are just as good as the parent.

Pennine Silk A very attractive shell pink with double flowers. Height 48in (120cm).

Red Wendy A deep red double flower that produces masses of blooms. Height 36in (90cm).

Spider / Spoons

Pennine Ace Pink / white. Height 42in (105cm).

Pennine Alfie A lovely bronze spoon. Height 42in (105cm).

Pennine Flute A lovely purple. Height 42in (105cm).

Pennine Jewel The flowers are a golden-bronze colour. Height 48in (120cm).

Anemone

Pennine Cadet A rich red. Height 48in (120cm).

Pennine Oriel Ray florets are of an oyster colour. Height 48in (120cm).

Pennine Poppet Pure white. Height 42in (105cm).

Pennine Rave Pink flowers. Height 42in (105cm).

Pennine Twinkle A canary yellow. Height 42in (105cm).

Tone Gold A rich copper bronze. Height 42in (105cm).

Sprays Flowering from Early September into October

Dee Ruby A purple-red double flower that is very attractive. Height 42in (105cm).

Embee Sunray A lovely yellow single that produces masses of blooms. Height 42in (105cm).

Gertrude The flowers are a delicate salmon-pink. Height 48in (120cm).

Karin An attractive colour of lilac. Height 42in (105cm).

Madeleine The double flowers are light pink in colour. Height 42in (105cm).

Margaret Deep pink double blooms that flower at a height of 42in (105cm). There is a wide range of sports in various colours from this cultivar. The 'Bronze' and 'Fleet Margaret' usually flower at the end of September.

Pennine Lotus An eye-catching cultivar with double flowers of creamy white blending into a lemon centre. Height 42in (105cm).

Pennine Spice Produces masses of orange double blooms that flower at a height of 42in (105cm).

Pennine Trinket A lovely double in deep rose with a gold reverse. Height 42in (105cm).

Late-Flowering Cultivars for the Cold Greenhouse

(These cultivars should be stopped during May or June to produce blooms for cut flowers during October and early November.)

Amy Shoesmith Pink incurving; requires stopping at the end of May. Height 60in (150cm).

Bagley Cream A cream incurve. Stop early May. Height 54in (135cm).

Cheddar A yellow incurve. Stop early May. Height 42in (105cm).

Peter White A pure white intermediate. Stop mid-May. Height 48in (120cm).

Linda Young A deep yellow medium flower of intermediate form. Stop early June. Height 60in (150cm).

October Harvest A light orange reflexed bloom. Stop mid-May. Height 48in (120cm).

West Bromwich A very nice white reflexed cultivar. Stop mid-May. Height 48in (120cm). There are two other sports of this cultivar in primrose and yellow.

EXHIBITION CULTIVARS FOR THE BEGINNER
Early-flowering Outdoor cultivars

Incurved

Cultivar	Section	Height	North	Central	South
			Stopping dates		
Buff Peter Rowe	23b Y	48in (1.2m)	25/4	1/5	10/5
Peter Rowe	23b Y	48in (1.2m)	25/4	1/5	10/5
Emma Lou	23a Y	54in (1.35m)	15/4	25/4	1/5
Winnie Bramley	23a Y	54in (1.35m)	5/5	10/5	15/5

Reflexed

Cultivar	Section	Height	North	Central	South
			Stopping dates		
Eve Gray	24b P	42in (1.05m)	25/5	25/5	1/6
Dorothy Gosling	24b P	42in (1.05m)	24/4	1/5	10/5
New Stylist	24b Y	54in (1.35m)	5/5	10/5	15/5
Susan Freestone	24b Y	48in (1.2m)	15/5	15/5	20/5
Venice	24b P	60in (1.5m)	25/4	1/5	10/5
Apricot Courtier	24a LB	54in (1.35m)	1/5	10/5	15/5
Courtier	24a P	54in (1.35m)	1/5	10/5	15/5
Gambit	24a P	48in (1.2m)	15/5	20/5	1/6

Intermediate

Cultivar	Section	Height	North	Central	South
			Stopping dates		
Cornish	25b Cr	36in (90cm)	25/4	5/5	15/5
Gingernut	25b LB	48in (1.2m)	5/5	15/5	20/5
Keystone	25b Pu	48in (1.2m)	25/5	25/5	1/6
Mac's Delight	25b Y	54in (1.35m)	15/4	24/4	1/5
Murial Vipas	25b W	48in (1.2m)	10/4	25/4	10/5
Ann Dickson	25a LB	60in (1.5m)	15/4	5/5	15/5
Deva Glow	25a Y	54in (1.35m)	25/4	5/5	15/5
Bill Wade	25a W	54in (1.35m)	1/4	20/4	1/5
Primrose Bill Wade	25a PY	54in (1.35m)	10/4	15/4	10/5
Pink World of Sport	25a P	48in (1.2m)	25/4	1/5	10/5

Early-Flowering Sprays

Cultivar	Section	Height	North	Central	South
			Stopping dates		
Anna Marie	29c W	36in (90cm)	20/5	25/5	1/6
Broadway Mandy	29c LP	54in (1.35m)	15/5	25/5	1/6
Dee Darkeye	29b OC	36in (90cm)	15/5	25/5	30/5
Dee Lemon	29c LY	36in (90cm)	15/5	25/5	1/6
Enbee Wedding	29d LP	48in (1.2m)	15/5	25/5	30/5
Madeleine	29c P	42in (1.05m)	20/5	1/6	10/6
Margaret	29c P	48in (1.2m)	1/5	15/5	25/5
Pennine Ace	29f P	42in (1.05m)	15/5	20/5	30/5
Pennine Flute	29f Pu	42in (1.05m)	15/5	20/5	30/5
Pennine Gambol	29a LP	36in (90cm)	15/5	20/5	1/6
Pennine Magic	29c LY	42in (1.05m)	15/5	25/5	1/6
Purple Pennine Wine	29c Pu	42in (1.05m)	1/6	10/6	15/6
Pennine Silk	29c LP	48in (1.2m)	15/5	25/5	1/6
Pennine Soldier	29d R	42in (1.05m)	15/5	25/5	1/6
Red Wendy	29c R	36in (90cm)	10/5	25/5	6/6
Tone Sail	29a Cr	36in (90cm)	10/5	25/5	5/6
Talbot Bolero	29c R	36in (90cm)	1/5	15/5	25/5

Late-Flowering Cultivars

Large Exhibition

Cultivar	Section	Height	Stopping dates		
			North	*Central*	*South*
Duke of Kent	1 W	48in (1.2m)	10/5	15/5	20/5
Gigantic	1 OC	72in (1.8m)	10/5	15/5	25/5
Harry Gee	1 P	48in (1.2m)	N.B.	N.B.	N.B.
Jessie Habgood	1 W	54in (1.35m)	5/5	10/5	15/5

Medium Exhibition

Cultivar	Section	Height	Stopping dates		
			North	*Central*	*South*
Cossack	2 R	48in (1.2m)	N.B.	N.B.	N.B.
Doug Cottam	2 Pu	60in (1.5m)	5/5	15/5	25/5
Idris	2 S	42in (1.05m)	25/5	1/6	10/6
Lundy	2 W	66in (1.65m)	25/5	1/6	10/6

Incurved

Cultivar	Section	Height	Stopping dates		
			North	*Central*	*South*
Fairweather	3b P	42in (1.05m)	10/5	15/5	25/5
John Hughes	3b W	54in (1.35m)	N.B.	25/5	1/6
Minstrel Boy	3b B	60in (1.5m)	1/6	10/6	20/6
Stockton	3b Pu	54in (1.35m)	15/5	20/5	30/5
Shirley Model	3a P	54in (1.35m)	N.B.	15/5	20/5
Shirley Sunburst	3a Y	66in (1.65m)	N.B.	15/5	20/5

Reflexed

Cultivar	Section	Height	Stopping dates		
			North	*Central*	*South*
Olwyn	4b W	60in (1.5m)	25/5	1/6	10/6
Patricia Millar	4b LP	54in (1.35m)	1/6	10/6	15/6
Tom Stilwell	4b LY	66in (1.65m)	5/6	15/6	25/6
Sefton	4a R	72in (1.8m)	20/5	1/6	10/6
Riley's Dynasty	14a P	54in (1.35m)	1/6	10/6	20/5
West Bromwich	14a W	54in (1.35m)	7/6	20/6	25/6

(The last two cultivars should be rooted in early March for the stopping dates given.)

Intermediates

Cultivar	Section	Height	Stopping dates		
			North	*Central*	*South*
Crown Derby	5b LB	42in (1.05m)	1/6	15/6	25/6
Denton Delight	5b LY	48in (1.2m)	25/5	5/6	15/6
Roy Coopland	5b Lb	66in (1.65m)	20/5	1/6	10/6
Winter Queen	5b W	84in (2.1m)	1/5	15/5	25/5
Alexis	5a P	54in (1.35m)	15/5	20/5	1/6
Charles Tandy	5a W	54in (1.35m)	25/5	1/6	10/6
Beacon	5a R	60in (1.5m)	15/5	25/5	6/6
Sam Vinter	5a W	60in (1.5m)	15/5	25/5	1/6

Anemones

Cultivar	Section	Height	Stopping dates		
			North	*Central*	*South*
Rolinda	6b LB	48in (1.2m)	1/4–1/6	10/4–10/6	15/4–15/6
Thora	6b P	54in (1.35m)	1/4–7/6	10/4–10/6	15/4–14/6
Marion Stacey	6a Pu	54in (1.35m)	1/4–1/6	10/4–10/6	15/4–15/6
Raymond Mounsey	6a R	48in (1.2m)	1/4–1/6	10/4–10/6	15/4–15/6

Singles

Cultivar	Section	Height	Stopping dates		
			North	*Central*	*South*
Chesswood Beauty	7b R	60in (1.5m)	N.B.	15/4–15/6	20/4–20/6
Hedgerow	7b P	48in (1.2m)	1/4–20/5	15/4–15/6	20/4–20/6
Mason's Bronze	7b B	60in (1.5m)	N.B.	15/4–15/6	20/4–20/6
Woolman's Glory (and its sports)	7a B	54in (1.35m)	1/4–25/5	10/4–1/6	15/4–10/6

All the stopping dates given are for shows in either early September, or late October to early November. For show dates later in September or November the dates given will have to be adjusted.

Glossary

Anemone Similar to the single flower type, except the central disc has small tubular florets forming a raised cushion, and usually only one row of petals.

Cultivar A variety of chrysanthemum (the term is used internationally).

Cutting A short length of basal growth used to produce a plant almost identical to the original.

Incurve A bloom whose petals curve upwards forming a neat ball.

Intermediate A bloom which is similar to the incurve, but which has an open texture with the petals not closing over at the apex.

Large and medium exhibition Often referred to as Japs, usually grown one up and either of an incurving or a reflexing form.

Lateral The stem on which the flower will bloom.

Natural break (Sometimes shown as 'N.B.') When the growing tip of the plant forms a bud naturally, and laterals start to grow from the axil joints of the leaves on the main stem.

Plant breeders' rights Rights owned by the plant breeder when a variety is registered, meaning that the variety can only be sold by the breeder or one of his outlets. The variety may or may not be registered for exhibition.

Pompon Type with blooms that are small, perfectly round balls of florets, varying in size from ½–2in (1–5cm).

Pre-budding   The short length of lateral growth used for reproduction forms a bud.

Reflex   A bloom where the petals curve downwards or horizontal to the stem.

Registered   When a variety has been recorded as an exhibition variety and placed in a section indicating whether it is either an early, mid-season or late-flowering chrysanthemum. It is then shown in the NCS register.

Single   A daisy-type flower that may have one single row or several rows of petals, in each case displaying a centre disc.

Spoon   A single bloom in appearance, with one or more rows of petals which are tubular for two-thirds of their length and open out at the end to give a spoon effect.

Stool   The root and a short length of flowering stem at the end of the flowering period.

Stop, second stop   Removal of the growing tip, and then of the growing tips of the laterals.

Timing   Method by which the natural flowering date of a cultivar can be adjusted.

Index

Other gardening titles available from The Crowood Press:

Dahlias
The Complete Guide   Philip Damp
ISBN 1 85223 052 5

Delphiniums
The Complete Guide   Colin Edwards
ISBN 1 85223 150 5

Fuchsias
The Complete Guide to Cultivation, Propagation and
Exhibition   George Bartlett
ISBN 1 85223 029 0

Geraniums and Pelargoniums
The Complete Guide to Cultivation, Propagation and
Exhibition   Jan Taylor
ISBN 1 85223 034 7